Becoming Human Again

A Biblical Primer on Entire Sanctification
by Timothy Crutcher

Cover Design: Brianna Yates-Grantz and Alyssa McWilliams
Interior Design: Brianna Yates-Grantz

For Darrik Acre-

friend, pastor, encourager, and fellow pilgrim on this road

Contents

Foreword

I am an unapologetic son of the American Holiness Movement. My father joined the Church of the Nazarene at the time of the 25th Anniversary of the denomination. On my wall is the diploma granted him on his graduation from the Theological College department of Trevecca Nazarene College in 1941. My mother is a graduate of Asbury College. I grew up in the deep south in the Church of the Nazarene and am a graduate of Trevecca and Nazarene Theological Seminary. I have spent the entirety of my ministry in the Church of the Nazarene, serving as a pastor and as an administrator. I know our theology. It has been my life and breath for the last 60 years.

But I also know our vulnerability in regard to our theology. Over the last century we have wrestled with how to best articulate the doctrine of Christian holiness, the distinguishing tenet of the Church of the Nazarene. We, along with our sisters and brothers in other holiness denominations, have worked hard to make the message relevant, accessible, and understandable. But we have also spent much relational capital in our arguments with one another as to what this message really means.

The early American holiness people were clear in their understanding that they were the sons and daughters of John Wesley. But they also felt themselves responsible for some necessary corrections that, to a great measure, democratized the Wesleyan movement. One tendency that developed was to ground the message in the experience of entire sanctification. While such an experience may be valid, it must never be the authoritative measure of holiness. Holiness must be grounded in the nature and character of God. Any experience of sanctification we may enjoy is not the final authority. Any measure of holiness we display is at best derivative. The norm is not our experience. The norm is the love of God expressed in the gift of His Son. It is in the sacrificial, suffering love demonstrated in the life, teachings, death, and resurrection of Jesus of Nazareth.

In this wonderful book you will find a refreshing articulation of the message of holiness. It is readable, accessible, and insightful. Tim Crutcher has the mind of a scholar, the heart of a pastor, and the humility of an honest disciple seeking to know the Truth. I believe he offers a meaningful and contemporary explanation and exposition of the Wesleyan holiness message for a new generation. It is founded on Scripture and a deep appreciation for the character of the God who is in and of himself the expression of holiness, the measure of holiness, and the generous source of holiness for his creatures.

Jesse C. Middendorf
General Superintendent Emeritus
Church of the Nazarene

Introduction

The doctrine of entire sanctification seems to have fallen on some hard times in recent years. Fifty years ago, most people who attended a "Holiness" church could have told you what sanctification meant because they heard it preached on regularly. Churches even held special revival services in which the proclamation about—and invitation to—entire sanctification was the whole point. The publishing houses of these churches, too, would produce many books on holiness and sanctification, and people would buy and read them. Looking back, it seemed like sanctification was the topic to talk about. Nowadays, however, fewer people seem to want to preach on the doctrine, and not all of those agree on what we should say. Fewer books are written and read, and it sometimes seems like one can attend a historical "Holiness" church and not hear about holiness at all.

Some of this decline in interest in entire sanctification happened because too many people who talked about holiness talked about it in terms of rules—"Don't drink, don't chew, don't hang with those who do"—and those rules became stifling. Some of the decline is due to the fact that people would testify to being "entirely sanctified" on Sunday in church, but they would not necessarily lead lives others would recognize as holy, and the disconnect made talking about holiness uncomfortable. Some explanations of entire sanctification sounded rote and mechanical, like it was simply the next thing that happened when you had an emotional encounter with God after you had been saved, and that made it hard to see why it mattered. Once people were saved, they were going to heaven, right? So why bother with whatever comes after? However it happened, the doctrine of entire sanctification is often found neglected on the margins in many churches where it was once front and center. There are even some folks in these churches who have never heard about it at all.

This book is a plea for Holiness Churches to start taking entire sanctification as seriously as they used to, and it was written with the goal of helping to jump-start that conversation. The book is constructed as a primer for beginners, a course in "Holiness 101," as it were. Like all primers, it is designed to be a helpful first word on a subject rather than the last one, a book that encourages one to read more books. This book offers one approach to the "logic" of holiness, how it works and how it connects to the rest of the Christian faith. Hopefully, that will empower people to seek out and read other explorations of holiness, from the classics of the Holiness Tradition to those yet-unwritten books on holiness that would emerge if churches started taking the doctrine more seriously again.

This book is also a biblical primer, one designed to help the reader see how entire sanctification is woven through the warp and woof of Scripture. Far from being an odd "add on" to the Gospel that a few quirky churches decided to emphasize, sanctification is what the Gospel is all about. Far from being something reserved for spiritual elites, sanctification is an ordinary reality in Scripture, forming the background of many of the laws and stories and songs and prophecies that comprise the biblical testimony. In fact, a careful reading of the Bible reveals that holiness is what God made humanity for in the first place, which is why we can approach it as a way of Becoming Human Again. Given the role that Scripture plays in this book—frequently cited but only occasionally quoted—many readers will find it helpful to have a Bible (or Bible app) available as they read.

We will approach the task of exploring entire sanctification by giving it a long introduction. We will begin by laying out the basic vocabulary of the discussions, drawing some distinctions that will be helpful as our conversations continue. From that point, we will do a little "crash course" in Christian thinking: what is God like, what are human beings like, what fell apart between human beings and God, and how does

God go about fixing that. This long introduction will take us most of the way through the book, but there is no other way to truly understand entire sanctification. By building the doctrine from the ground up, we can see how the top pieces are supported by all the pieces underneath. Finally, we will explore the idea of entire sanctification itself, trace a few of its implications for the Christian life, and then we will be finished.

While this primer is primarily directed toward helping people understand sanctification, we all recognize the uselessness of truth that merely sits in our heads or on a shelf. Unless we put truth to work in our own lives, it does not matter what we know. This is what the Bible means by wisdom, figuring out what God is like and how the world works so that we can live well with God in that world. This book functions best if it is read more as an invitation to wisdom than as a collection of ideas. Its real goal is to invite people into the reality of sanctification, not merely to tell people about it. It's a trail map much more than a travelogue, an invitation to a journey more than a report about one, and our prayer is that God uses it that way in the lives of its readers.

Chapter One

The Concept of Holiness

Our first step on the journey to understand holiness and sanctification is to get a sense of the words we will use along the way. All cultures and religions have an idea of holiness, so the concept is not unique to the Christian faith. Christians, however, use the word in a distinctive way. If we understand the basic idea, we can better understand the ways in which Christians have transformed this universal concept into a central confession of their faith.

Human beings are naturally religious creatures, and most people throughout history have believed in something transcendent, something beyond the world we see, hear, touch, taste, and smell. From Jews, Muslims, and Sikhs to Buddhists, Taoists, and Hindus, religious people recognize that our physical world is not all there is to reality. When people point to this transcendent world, no matter what language they are speaking, they will use a word we can translate into English as "holy." The word "holy" describes people, places, and things in this world that point to that world beyond. Buddhists may describe a monk as holy because his calm and placid demeanor reminds them of Nirvana, a state free of all passions. Muslims will not allow non-Muslims to enter the Dome of the Rock in Jerusalem because it is a holy place, and non-believers have no business there. An African shaman might have a holy drum that he uses to contact the ancestor spirits, and it would be unthinkable to use that same drum to make music for an ordinary gathering. No matter the religion, if people believe in a transcendent reality that connects to ours, they will describe that connection as "holy."

For Christians, however, the word is more than a useful reminder of the transcendent. For those who claim to follow Jesus, the word is also an invitation. Jesus invited his disciples into a pattern of knowing and becoming like God that fosters deeper knowledge and clearer likeness. This likeness is to show up in our actions in such a way that others "may see your good deeds and glorify your Father in heaven" (Mt 5:16). Jesus does not limit this invitation to a small, select group of people; it is an invitation to all who would claim the title of Christian. We cannot hear this invitation, however, if we do not understand the words through which it is extended. Unfortunately, especially among churches that call themselves "Holiness Churches," many of the words associated with this invitation—words like "holiness," "sanctification," and "perfection"—have had their meanings dulled and damaged through misuse. Sometimes they have created more confusion than clarity, more fear than hope. By refreshing our understanding of these terms, we can learn to hear them again as Scripture intended.

To some people, fussing about vocabulary sounds nit-picky and unnecessary, and perhaps that is often the case. However, if we want to have a common conversation about something, we have to have a common language for it. People do not always hear words the way we intend them, especially with topics like entire sanctification that tend to generate disagreement. We cannot unite ourselves around a Christian identity rooted in holiness and be a "Holiness People" if we cannot find that common language. If "sanctification" sounds confusing or contradictory, there is no reason to talk about it—let alone commit one's life to it.

Clarifying our language, then, is the first step toward re-invigorating this conversation and rediscovering how important this concept has been, and still can be, for us. Our words matter, so it is worth the time to explore them in depth.

The Idea of the Holy

What does it mean to say that something is holy? Our English word "holy" seems to come from the same root from which we get "hale," "whole," and "healthy." The original word (*halig* in Old English) referred to something uncorrupted. The world of the gods seemed free of the death and decay that plagues our world, so it was a good word to describe the difference between the transcendent world and ours. Once Christians got to the British Isles, they started using the English word "holy" to translate two Latin ideas: 1) *sanctus*, meaning "dedicated" or "confirmed" (from which we get "sanctified"), and 2) *sacer*, meaning "set apart for the gods" (from which we get "sacred"). Once associated with God (or the gods), however, adjectives like "holy" and "sanctified" and "sacred" work differently from other descriptive words we use.

We often say "holy" means "set apart," but it means more than that. If we set apart a field for playing football or set apart a chair for Dad's exclusive use, we would not call that a holy field or a holy chair. To be holy is more than to be set apart; it is to be set apart *for God*. To set a person, place, or thing apart as holy is to recognize, as we noted above, that it points to the transcendent world. Other descriptive words like "blue," "soft," or "loud" are meaningful because they point to things in our experience. By contrast, the word "holy" is meaningful because it points beyond our experience. A holy place reminds us of the divine, a place we might expect to encounter God. A holy object is something set apart for service to God and should never be used for secular purposes. A holy person is someone who reminds us of God, a person who somehow embodies in this world the presence of the world beyond.

Because "holy" points beyond our experience, its meaning is evocative much more than descriptive, which is why people use it when they swear. When used properly, however, it kindles feelings of awe and reverence, pointing to the overlap between God's reality and our own but not really telling us much about it. To label something as holy is to say there is something about it that we cannot quite capture by our language, something beyond our understanding. There are divine qualities like power and love that we can describe, but the word "holy" makes us realize that we do not fully understand them. God's holy love must be more than human love, and it will always be somewhat mysterious to us. God's holy power has a quality no earthly power can ever approach.

All discussions about holiness begin with the recognition that the word "holy" is an otherworldly word. We cannot start with a worldly understanding of the word and then decide how it applies to God. We start with God because "holy" means "God-like." It is not our understanding of "holy" that helps us to describe God; it is our understanding of God that fills out what we mean when we call something "holy." This means we have to be careful when we use the word to describe things that are not God. Strictly speaking, the word "holy" only applies to God. "Holy" means "God-like" and there is no one like God. Applied to God, the word "holy" makes sense. Applied to anything else, the word "holy" must come with disclaimers and asterisks. Nothing else and no one else reflects all of God's qualities the way God does. As we often sing:

> Only Thou art holy
> There is none beside Thee,
> Perfect in power,
> In love and purity.[1]

Yes, there are times when something of God is known and felt, and we can rightly describe such times as holy moments and holy encounters. There are people whose lives reflect enough of God for us to recognize them as holy people. We can and do use the word "holy" to refer to things that are not God, but we do so tentatively, always keeping in mind its derivative sense. So, just as we might describe as

---

1 Reginald Heber, "Holy, Holy, Holy! Lord God Almighty!" 1826.

"father-like" the loving actions of someone who is not a father, we can describe as "God-like" the actions and attitudes of someone who is not God. The difference is subtle, but it is one we must keep in mind. No matter how holy a human person might become, there will always be a gap—an infinite gap—between a holy person and The Holy God.

Holiness and Sanctification

Thus far, we have dealt with the adjective "holy." What happens when we turn this descriptive word into a noun? What does it mean to talk about "holiness"? Is that a thing? Can human beings possess that thing? And how does this relate to the other noun we often use in this discussion: "sanctification"? Given how often we will be using those words in this book, it is worth our time to get them straight.

Our English word "sanctification" comes from the Latin *sanctus*, and the English word "holy" was used to translate that Latin idea. So, although the words look very different, the ideas of holiness and sanctification have been linked for as long as Christians have been speaking English. However, while the English adjective "holy" and the Latin adjective *sanctus* have similar meanings, there is an important difference between the nouns we derive from them. We often use the words "holiness" and "sanctification" interchangeably, but that obscures an important feature of their formation. Understanding the difference between them helps us maintain the distinction between God's holy nature and the way that nature is displayed through people and things that are not God but are still "God-pointing" or "God-like."

The word "holiness" is simple and straightforward. We take our adjective "holy" and we add to it a suffix ("-ness") that turns it directly into a noun. "Holy-ness" means "the quality of being holy." It is a static word, and like the adjective "holy," it refers to an unchanging quality of God's nature. This might be experienced in direct encounters with God, or it could be reflected by people or things in the world, but it is something that only God possesses.

The word "sanctification" is a bit more complicated. First, we take our Latin adjective *sanctus* and turn it into an action word: the verb "sanctify." We do this all the time when we want to refer to the process by which a quality is instilled into a thing. We "realize" our dreams when we take our dreams and make them real. We "verify" a statement when we engage in a process that demonstrates the statement as true (*verus*, in Latin). So, when we "sanctify" something, we engage in a process that makes it *sanctus*, "holy." We then turn the verb "sanctify" into the noun "sanctification" to refer to that process. So, where holiness is a static idea, sanctification is a dynamic one. It refers to an activity, something that happens in time and isn't true from the start. To put it another way, holiness is about "*being holy*" but sanctification is about "*becoming holy*."[2]

We need not be fussy about this distinction, but knowing about it helps us in two ways. First, we can use the difference between "holiness" and "sanctification" to help us keep track of the direct and derivative uses of the word "holy" whenever that becomes important. God is holy by nature; we are not. There are times when we need to be clear about the holiness that is God's alone and the sanctification that God wants to instill in us.

Second, God's holiness is a given quality; our sanctification is not. There was never a time when God was not holy, but there was a time when we were not sanctified. Strictly speaking, God does not become holy; God is always that way. Strictly speaking, we cannot be holy; we can only become more and more like God. God's characteristics may be displayed through us, but they do not belong to us any more than the image in a mirror belongs to the mirror. When we need to remind ourselves of these realities, we can use the difference between "holiness" and "sanctification" to do that.

Holiness and Perfection

There is one final important idea that we must clarify before we move on, and that is the idea of perfection. We often label discussions about entire sanctification as discussions about Christian

---

2 When human beings set something apart for God as holy, English translations of the Bible will often use another word, "consecrate," to refer to that activity instead of "sanctify." That is almost always a stylistic variation in English. The word in the original languages of the Scripture is the one translated elsewhere as "sanctify." The few exceptions translate a word that literally means "purposed," with the implication that this is "purposed for God."

perfection, and that identification has a long history. Jesus himself links the two concepts when he translates God's call in the Old Testament to "Be holy because I am holy" (Lev. 11:45, 19:2, and quoted in 1 Pet 1:16) into "Be perfect as your Heavenly Father is perfect" (Mt 5:48). John Wesley's most famous book on sanctification was called *A Plain Account of Christian Perfection*. So, one of the questions we will be exploring throughout this book is the question of how "becoming holy"—looking like and pointing to God—relates to the biblical idea of being "perfect."

The best way to understand the biblical concept of perfection is to see what it does *not* mean. We often misunderstand Christian perfection because of the way we tend to use the word "perfect" in English. We get our English word "perfect" from the Latin *perfectus*, from the verb *perficere*, meaning "to finish or complete." So, we think that if something is "perfect," it is finished, complete, as-good-as-it-gets-and-can't-get-any-better. All of that is well and good, except when we use this word to translate a biblical word that means something different.

When Jesus says, "Be perfect as your Heavenly Father is perfect," he does not use a word that means what *perficere* means. To our English ears, it sounds like Jesus is saying, "Be unchangeably-as-good-as-you-can-ever-be as your Heavenly Father is unchangeably-as-good-as-God-is," but that is not what he is saying. The word Jesus uses (τέλειος, *teh-lay-os*, in Greek) has the connotation of "complete" or "brought to its end goal," but the word is better translated "mature" than "perfect." To our ears, perfection means "can't get better," but maturity is always a moving target.

We may observe the behavior of a five-year-old girl and say to ourselves, "Wow, that's a mature five-year-old." If we do, we mean something like this: "We can't imagine a five-year-old acting any better than she is acting." However, if we were to observe the exact same behavior in an eighteen-year-old, we probably would not say that the eighteen-year-old was acting mature. As we will see, this recognition helps us avoid confusion about what God does and does not do in sanctification. If we think "Christian Perfection" means "we are as Christian as we can ever get and can't get any better," then we might think that entire sanctification means we are "perfectly holy" and God is basically finished with us. However, if we hear the phrase "Christian perfection" as "Christian maturity," then we can see that entire sanctification—for all that it represents a major transition in our spiritual lives—can be compatible with continued growth in grace, just as we expect even someone who is a mature forty-year-old to continue to become more mature as she grows older.[3]

So, "holy" and "holiness" refer primarily to God's nature and character and secondarily to the way that nature is reflected through some of the things and people that God has made. "Sanctification" refers to the process by which people and things and places are set apart for God. This "setting apart" both empowers a deeper relationship to God and enables them to point to God more effectively. "Perfection" in the biblical sense means "maturity," the goal of becoming a full person after the image of God, becoming truly human again. Now that we have a basic grasp of these words, we are ready to fill them out with deeper and more substantive content. Since none of those words has any meaning apart from our understanding of God, it is to the task of describing this Holy God that we now turn.

---

3 Tom Noble captures this nicely in the subtitle to his book *Holy Trinity: Holy People: A Theology of Christian Perfecting* (Eugene, OR: Cascade, 2013). By switching from "perfection" to "perfecting," Noble captures the sense that this finishing work is always an ongoing reality.

Chapter Two

The Holy God

Since the word "holy" means "God-like," holiness begins with the nature and character of God. True holiness is God's alone, and it is only associated with not-God entities (people, places, and things) in a derivative sense (God-*like*). The direct and derivative senses of the word, however, can easily become confused. One problem with discussions about holiness is that they have been focused on things other than God. Human moral and cultural behavior are important to discussions about sanctification, but they are secondary. If we want to talk about behaviors related to drugs or entertainment or clothing or jewelry, we should always be able to draw a direct line between the way holiness is reflected in human behavior and the God who defines what holiness is.

Of course, if we were to cover everything God has revealed about Godself, "even the whole world would not have room for the books that would be written" (Jn 21:25). So, in this chapter on God we will confine ourselves to three ideas that are important for understanding God's work of sanctification. First, we will consider how a Christian belief in One True God allows the idea of holiness to have a definite meaning, something more than the vague confession, "This has something to do with the divine." Next, we will look at the way God creates and relates to the world so that it is possible for things in the world to become reflections of God's holy character. Finally, we will touch on that key characteristic of God that God most desires to put on display: love.

The One True God

It is a simple but often unappreciated confession: "There is only one God." One of the most important verses in all of the Old Testament is Deuteronomy 6:4, often known by its first word in Hebrew: "The *Shema*." Time and time again, Israel would repeat, "Hear, O Israel. The LORD our God, the LORD is one."

The word we translate "LORD" in capital letters is the name under which God revealed Godself to Israel: "Yahweh." Yahweh is God, and Yahweh is the only one to whom the word "God" can point. This means that other God-pointing words like "holy" point only to this particular God. There may be other things in the spiritual world beyond our physical one (heaven, angels, etc.), but those things can be called "holy" only in the same derivative sense that any created thing can be holy.

For Christians and Jews, then, "holy" means more than simply "religious." The word does not point vaguely to a spiritual world but to the personal and moral character of the One True God. This idea is central to Israel's faith, and it separated Israel's religion from all the religions that surrounded them. When God called Abraham out of Ur of the Chaldees (Gen 12), everyone else was following a more or less predictable religious pattern. While some people got the idea that there could be a single divine entity somewhere behind all reality, religious practices were directed toward a variety of different gods and goddesses who governed various aspects of nature and human experience. We usually call this form of religion "polytheism."

In the ancient world, people explained the often chaotic world in which we live by correlating its happenings to the happenings of a mythical transcendent world. This physical world, they felt, was created to serve that spiritual one, and it reflected "down here" whatever happened "up there." That mythical world was inhabited by numerous gods and goddesses, and they did not always get along. There were gods of war and goddesses of love competing for allegiance. There were gods of the sky and goddesses of harvest, and their interaction is what made crops grow. There were gods of the sea, gods of the dead, and gods of the various nations, and all of them affected human life. The number and names of these divine beings differed from culture to culture, as did the stories they told about them, but the basic pattern was the same. If the gods became angry "up there," bad things would happen "down here." Conversely, though, if one could keep the gods happy through worship and sacrifices, then good things would happen instead.

While this way of thinking assumes a strong connection between our world and the world of the gods, it allows for only a vague understanding of holiness. To most ancient people, the world of the gods functioned very much like the world we live in. The values, motivations, and attitudes that shaped divine activity sounded like the ones that shape ours. Gods were described like human rulers, only more powerful; they differed from us in degree but not in kind. They had ambitions and desires, their plans could fail, they could be manipulated by flattery, and they liked to be well-fed. They also got jealous and fought amongst themselves, and the chaos they created in their world filtered down into our own.

If one has a bunch of gods competing with each other for power or worship, the word "holy" has only a narrow and limited use. One can use it for temples, priests, altars and the like, but it does not say much more than, "This points to the gods." It is a ceremonial and religious idea, but it cannot be a personal or moral one. The gods themselves do not always behave morally, and what might count as a virtue with one god would be a vice when viewed from another god's perspective. The goddess of the hearth and home, say, would appreciate a father's dedication to his family and his refusal to go to war, but the god of war would see that very devotion as intolerable cowardice. In such a world, religion rarely connects well to virtue and behavior. Each god governs his or her own little set of values. Since those values often conflict, the word "holy" cannot point to any one of them. If we say "holy" means "god-like," we must first ask "Which god is that like?" A place that is "holy" to the goddess of love would not have much in common with a place "holy" to the god of war.

Because of the way God revealed Godself to Israel, they saw all such religions as "idolatry." Using the divine world to explain our world always ends up creating the divine world in our image, whether those images are physically crafted as idols or only exist in our heads as ideas. Israel's experience of their God Yahweh was first and foremost an experience of an "Other," of One who is not like us at all. Their "Holy Other" was "wholly other," completely set apart, distinct and different.

We can see this as far back as God's call on Abraham (Gen 12 and 17). Abraham is not out seeking God or looking for a way to explain his world. Instead, God comes to him and offers him much more of an invitation than an explanation. It is an invitation to leave the place he knows and follow this Yahweh God someplace else. Where polytheists were often trying to get the gods to do things, Israel understood God as trying to get them to do things. The first movement is God's, not humanity's. The same thing is true when God comes to rescue Israel from Egypt. It is God who calls Moses, God who engineers the events, God who comes from the world beyond into the world in which we live. That leads the Israelites to recognize right away, "Who among the gods is like you, LORD [Yahweh]? Who is like you—majestic in holiness, awesome in glory, working wonders?" (Ex 15:11).

In fact, the Scriptures will often emphasize how great the gulf is between our world and God. Isaiah goes on a long comparison between Yahweh and the so-called gods of the idolatrous religions in Isaiah 40. They are the products of human hands and thoughts, but Yahweh is the Holy One far above our world. Eventually, God speaks for Godself and says, "'For my thoughts are not your thoughts, neither are your ways my ways,' declares the LORD. 'As the heavens are higher than the earth, so are my ways higher than your ways and my thoughts than your thoughts'" (Is 55:8-9). Similar thoughts are expressed in other places (Mic 7:18-20, Pss 77:13 and 113:5-6). This is "God Almighty." There are no other divine powers or beings in that transcendent realm but God alone, and this God works in mysterious ways. We can point to God with a word like "holy," but this God will always be beyond us.

That said, God has still revealed some things to humanity about God's nature. Because the word "holy" points only to this One True God, it takes on the revealed characteristics and virtues of the One to whom it points. There are moral implications to the word "holy" because some actions line up with God's character and other actions do not, and God expects God's followers to act in ways that reflect God's nature. God does not come to Abraham like one of the gods of polytheism and say, "Give me what I want and I'll give you what you want." God says, "Walk before me faithfully and be blameless" (Gen 17:1). God offers to be the God of Abraham's descendants (Gen 17:8), but that places on them an obligation to live in holy ways that reflect God's character and God's priorities. If we label something as "holy" that does not point to God's faithful and consistent nature, we misuse the word.

One can see this in the various ways Israel uses the concept of holiness in its derivative sense as a label for things that point to God. As in other religions, Israel understood certain people, places, and things to be important for conducting the ceremonies and rituals that oriented the community toward God. Places like the "Holy of Holies" in the heart of the Temple were places reserved for God alone. Priests could be considered holy in the sense that their work was human work that was dedicated to God and that embodied God's work in the world. Even objects like the Ark of the Covenant could be deemed holy and thus could only be used in God's service.

However, the idea of the "holy" was still anchored in the character of God, and so there were things that could not be called "holy" and devoted to God. There is no such thing as a "holy idol," for example. Aaron's Golden Calf was explicitly designed to represent the "God who brought you up out of Egypt" and was used in a festival dedicated to Yahweh (Ex 32:4-5), but that didn't matter. That "holy idol" earned Israel Yahweh's wrath, not Yahweh's favor. There could also be nothing like a "holy prostitute," as there were in fertility religions. Certain things or people could not be designated as holy because they did not line up with the character of God.

Furthermore, Israel understood that even objects properly designated as "holy" were only effective in helping people orient themselves toward God; they did not bind God in any way. God could show up to protect such objects (2 Sam 6:7) but God could also let them go (as God did with the Temple [Ez 8-10]). Holy objects in other religions might be used to get the gods to act, but Israel learned that its holy objects had no power over God. When Israel tries to use the Ark—a holy object if ever there was one—to get God to fight for them against the Philistines, God simply lets the Ark be captured (1 Sam 4:1-11).

However, as important as the ceremonial uses of the word "holy" were, they were secondary to the way in which God's "holy people" lived. It did not matter if people used holy things if they led unholy lives. In Isaiah, God has no tolerance for this mismatch. God likens the people of Israel to Sodom and Gomorrah—the most sinful nations they could think of—and says to them:

> "The multitude of your sacrifices—what are they to me?" says the LORD. "I have more than enough of burnt offerings, of rams and the fat of fattened animals; I have no pleasure in the blood of bulls and lambs and goats. When you come to appear before me, who has asked this of you, this trampling of my courts? Stop bringing meaning less offerings!...Wash and make yourselves clean. Take your evil deeds out of my sight; stop doing wrong. Learn to do right; seek justice. Defend the oppressed. Take up the cause of the fatherless; plead the case of the widow." (Is 1:11-17)

Because Israel believed in the One True God, its understanding of holiness pointed to a God who is utterly beyond the world but whose character can still be seen in the world through holy objects and places and, most importantly, through a holy people. For Israel, and for Christians whose faith follows in their footsteps, holiness means more than a generic reference to the gods. It means pointing to the God of grace, compassion, justice, and love but doing so from within a world that is not itself divine. To see how that works, we must see how God works in and through the world that God made.

God and the World

If we believe in a God who is entirely distinct from the world—a Holy Other—but who still wants to be known in and through the world, we run into a dilemma. How can created and finite things reflect the character of the Uncreated, Infinite God? If we start with the world's capacity to reflect God, the idea seems nonsense. The gap between the finite and infinite, the created and uncreated is too great for anything on this side of the gap to bridge. So, we begin on the other side. God created a world specifically designed to reflect some of God's nature and character, and it is God's work that makes this possible. With that understanding, the idea begins to make sense.

The best place to see how God enables the world to point back to God is the story of creation. The truths of that story, however, stand out better if we once again compare Israel's beliefs with the polytheistic ones of the cultures around them. The myths of creation that they told were focused on explaining the physical world and its functions. In many of these stories, even the gods themselves were understood as products of vague and unexplained creative forces at work before the world itself existed. Usually, the creation of this world was the result of some prehistoric conflict between those primal creative forces and the gods who conquered them to create the ordered reality in which we live.[1] Many cultures added to these founding creation stories other myths that further explained how creation functioned, such as why there are seasons or why the sun appears to rise and set.

When we turn to the first chapter of Genesis, however, we find something very different. First of all, the story does not explain why things are the way they are. There are no interesting stories of fights or kidnappings to tell you why the world exists or why there is day or night or seasons. In fact, given that God is the One True God and there is nothing else around until God creates it, there could be no stories to tell. There are no problems to solve, no enemies to fight, no mythical world here at all—only God and God's creation of this physical world in which we live. The story in Genesis reveals much more about who God is and how God relates to creation than it does about why the world exists.

There are three things about God's work in creation that we need to recognize if we are going to understand God's work in sanctification, and we will treat each briefly in turn. First, we'll look at how God

---

1   So, for example, in Greek myths the god Zeus has to defeat his father Cronus the titan before he can command Prometheus and Epimetheus to make humankind and the animals. In the *Enuma Elish*, the Babylonian god Marduk has to defeat the chaos dragon Tiamat, and when he does so, he uses her body to fashion the world.

is both Creator and Empowerer, doing things that God's creatures cannot do but also empowering them to do things they could not do on their own. Second, we'll look at the fact that God created the world to be good, and that makes it capable of reflecting the goodness of God. Third, we'll look at the first time the word "holy" comes up in Scripture, and that is in reference to the creation of Sabbath.

God as Empowering Creator

Genesis begins with a simple affirmation that sets the stage for all of God's interactions with the world. "In the beginning, God created the heavens and the earth" (Gen 1:1). The verb here translated "create" (*bara'* in Hebrew) is a God-only activity because it represents the work of bringing something into being, a work only God can do. As we noted above, God does not have to fight to make the world or ask anyone's permission. God simply speaks and creation happens. There are no powers that oppose God because God has all the power that there is. God is "Almighty," or "omnipotent," to use the traditional theological word.[2]

Because God has this almighty, creative power, God's work requires no prerequisites or pre-conditions, and this is something we see throughout the Scripture. God can create the nation of Israel out of a band of slaves who have nothing to offer God (Ex 12-15). God can breathe life into dry bones that have no life in them at all (Ez. 37). God demonstrates this kind of creative power through Jesus when he gives sight to one who never had it before (Jn 9:1-7) and through Peter and John when they invited a man born lame to stand (Acts 3:1-7). One can even see it when Jesus multiplies the loaves and fishes to feed the five thousand (Mt 14:13-21). This unconditional power brings Jesus back from the dead and will eventually raise all those who follow him as well (Rom 8:10-11). Over and over again, the Bible affirms that God's work stands alone. This idea is important because sanctification is God's work. It is "wrought by God's grace,"[3] as the *Nazarene Manual* statement puts it, and so it is a creative work that doesn't depend on anything we might bring to the table.

---

2 From the Latin *omni* meaning "all" and *potentia* meaning "power."

3 *Manual*, 31.

This, however, is only half the story of God's power in Genesis 1. Even though God can act alone, God often chooses not to. God often acts through intermediaries, using that creative power to empower creation to do things. God begins creating by calling things like light and sky into being. When it comes to creating life, however, God takes a different approach. Instead of saying, "Let there be plants," God says, "Let the land produce vegetation." God does this again with the fish (Gen 1:20) and the animals (Gen 1:24). God could have brought life into being on God's own, but instead God empowers God's creation to be creative, working through it rather than around it or apart from it. God further reinforces this empowering work by commanding the fish and the human beings to "be fruitful and increase in number" (Gen 1:22, 28). God brings the first instances of life out of the water and the ground, but life continues because God gives living things the ability to procreate, reflecting God's creative nature in a small but nevertheless meaningful way. God even shares God's governing authority with the sun and the moon on the fourth day of creation (Gen 1:16) and with humanity on the sixth (Gen 1:28).

This helps us understand how creation becomes capable of reflecting the character of the Uncreated God, how holiness among created things is possible. It is God's work, and so it requires nothing from creation, but it is God's work in and through creation. God is creative, and when God empowers God's creation to be creative, it ends up looking a bit like God. God is holy, and so God can empower God's creation to become holy as well. God's work comes first, but God's work empowers creation to respond. That dynamic will drive our understanding of sanctification.

Creation as Good

A second way Genesis 1 lays the foundation for our understanding of holiness is by emphasizing that God's creation resembles its Creator in this respect: it is good. God spends the first two days of creation bringing heavenly realities—light and sky—into existence. On the third day, God begins to make concrete things, and an interesting pattern emerges. Each time God finishes an act of creation, God recognizes something important about it: "And God saw that it was good" (Gen 1:10, 12, 18, 21, 25).

In the biblical world, the concept of goodness—like the concept of holiness—is anchored in God.[4] So, when God looks at a created thing and sees that it is good, God is recognizing something of God's own nature in that thing. This may strike us as odd because the world around us does not always appear to be good. Philosophical Greeks in Jesus's day—especially those known as Gnostics—saw the physical world as evil and at odds with the spiritual world where good resided. In their view, the physical world was a mistake, the creation of some lesser divine being (usually called "the Demiurge") who didn't really know what he was doing. Since that day, there have always been those who viewed the physical world with suspicion, if not outright disdain. Even today, there are people who think that the good spiritual world and the bad physical world are always going to be at odds with each other. Such thinking would make sanctification impossible.

The Bible, however, will have none of that. The world is good because God is good. Even though the Bible tells the story of a Fall and admits that the world now is not as it was created to be, there is still an inherent goodness in the world itself. The world, even in its fallen state, is still capable of pointing toward God. As the Psalmist sings, "The heavens declare the glory of God; the skies proclaim the work of his hands" (Ps 19:1). Paul reaffirms this as well when he claims that God is known through God's handiwork (Rom 1:20). In fact, when God desires to fully reveal Godself to humanity, God becomes a fleshly, embodied, made-of-dust-like-the-rest-of-us human being in Jesus, an irrefutable demonstration of the compatibility between God's spiritual reality and our physical one.

Interestingly enough, when God finishes the entire creation, God gives the whole an even higher evaluation than God gave the parts: "God saw all that he had made, and it was very good" (Gen 1:31). The individual parts of creation are good but the whole thing all together is very good. That, too, tells us something about the way God's creation is designed to reflect God.

---

4 Jesus reflects this understanding when he responds to being called "Good Teacher" by saying, "Why do you call me good? ... No one is good--except God alone" (Mk 10:18, Lk 18:19).

We see more of God's nature in the way things work together than in individual things standing on their own. Creation reflects its Creator more by its interrelationships than it does by standing still. The goodness of creation has a dynamic quality to it. As the animals are "fruitful and multiply" and as humans "fill the earth and subdue it," we get the sense that the goodness of the world is designed to increase and get even better.

This recognition is important to us because we often find ourselves tempted by the Gnostic illusion. It's easy for us to think that physical things like our bodies or the decorations in our sanctuaries are hurdles and handicaps to our spiritual lives with God. Physicality seems to be more a hindrance to holiness than a help. We think that God is spiritual and so a holiness that points to God is going to be exclusively spiritual as well. The Bible, however, says otherwise. The stuff of creation is good—very good when it's all working together—and it is in that very physical stuff and the way it behaves that God wants to be recognized and encountered. Holiness is not an abstract spiritual quality; it is something we will find in the ordinary, concrete, good world in which we live.

Sabbath as Holy Rest

The third way the creation story helps us understand holiness is with the seventh day of creation, the Sabbath. Many ancient stories of creation finished with the creation of a temple, a holy place where the gods could dwell. In Israel's story, the whole of creation serves as God's temple, and on the seventh day God takes up God's residence in that temple, as it were, and sets the day apart as a recognition of that fact. "[On] the seventh day God...finished the work he had been doing; so on the seventh day he rested from all his work. Then God blessed the seventh day and made it holy, because on it he rested from all the work of creating that he had done" (Gen 2:2-3).[5]

---

5 The NIV translation says "By" instead of "On" at the beginning of the verse, and states that God "had finished" God's work, but this is misleading. The first word in Hebrew is the word for "on" and the finishing work of creation is the blessing and setting apart of the seventh day. So, it is more properly biblical to speak of a seven-day creation than a six-day one with sabbath as an afterthought.

God has just spent six days doing phenomenal, only-God-can-do-that kinds of things. Though God sometimes works through created agents, all the activity has been God's. The seventh day, however, is different. When God brings order to time, God does so by resting. That is something God's creatures can also do. The Hebrew word for rest is *shabat* (from which we get the word "sabbath"), and its basic meaning is "to stop" or "to cease." God ceases doing Godlike things, and then God blesses this rest and sets it apart in a way that points back to God. From the very beginning of the Scripture, holiness is associated with rest.

The creation story shows us how God empowers creation to do things, and these things reflect God's nature and character. However, God is not God because God gets things done. God's holiness is a reflection of who God is, a matter of *being* more than *doing*. Moses's face does not shine with God's glory because he saw God do some great act but merely because he spoke to God (Ex 34:29-35). Isaiah is not convicted of his and his people's sinfulness because God judges him but merely because he sees a Holy God "high and lifted up" (Is 6). God sanctifies the seventh day and orders all of creation to rest (Ex 20:8-11) as a way of reminding God's people that God is reflected in who they are more than in how much they accomplish. Becoming like God will result in acting like God, but the priority of being over doing is important. God's creation will never become Godlike by trying to do the things God does. In fact, when humanity tries to become like God by doing things, the result is the Fall (Gen 3).

Genesis 1 orients us to a God who creates a world designed to reflect the qualities of its Creator. God's work is the foundation for anything creation does, but creation is permeable to God's activity, allowing God to work through it in empowering ways. Creation is good in a way that bears the imprint of its Good Creator, and God desires to be seen through the very physicality that makes it so different from God. The work of God, however, flows out of the being of God. So God creates a sabbath rest for God's creation as a way of reminding it that its reflection of God will follow the same pattern. This pattern is most clearly exemplified by that attribute of God that is most reflectable by God's creation: love.

God Is Love

The One True God so transcends our world that our merely human language has no hope of adequately describing God's reality. Yet, for two thousand years, Christians have been comfortable with distilling all of that reality down to one simple word: love. Love is God's "reigning attribute,"[6] to use John Wesley's phrase, and that fact must be central to any discussion of sanctification.

Scripture has many different ways of portraying the loving character of God. It is love that motivates God to save Israel from Egypt (Ex 15:13, Deut 7:8-9) and to continually work for the good of that nation (1 Kgs 10:9, 2 Chr 9:8). Israel celebrates God's love in song (Pss 34:12, 47:4, 146:8) and relies on it as the source of hope (Is 43:4, Jer 31:3). God is portrayed like a faithful husband (Is 54:5, Jer 31:32, Ez 16:8), a caring mother (Is 49:15, Hos 11:1-4, Deut 32:11), and a loving Father (Ex 4:22-23, Ps 103:13, Mal 3:17). Jesus makes this last idea the central metaphor for understanding God's relationship to God's creation, urging his followers to pray to "Our Father in Heaven" (Mt 6:9).

All of these reflections reach their peak in the Johannine writings of the New Testament. The most popular memory verse in the Bible tells us, "For God so loved the world that he gave his one and only Son, that whoever believes in him shall not perish but have eternal life" (Jn 3:16). In the first epistle of John, we find the clearest and simplest expression of the idea. "Dear friends, let us love one another, for love comes from God. Everyone who loves has been born of God and knows God. Whoever does not love does not know God, because God is love" (1 Jn 4:7-8). For John, God not only exhibits loving behavior, God is the one and only source of the reality we call love. Everywhere love exists, it exists because God is empowering it and sharing it with God's creation.

---

6 John Wesley, *Explanatory Notes on the New Testament*, 2 vols (Kansas City: Beacon Hill Press of Kansas City, 1981), §1 John 4:8.

With the coming of Jesus as God in the flesh and with the advent of the Holy Spirit, Jesus's followers come to realize that God's very being is a community of love, a Trinity of Father, Son, and Holy Spirit. Love describes the dynamic of God's life as the Father pours into and empowers the Son and the Son responds and glorifies the Father and the Spirit is like the breath of life and love between them—a breath that God also breathes into us. That love finds its highest demonstration on the cross, where God's self-emptying, self-sacrificing love redeems humanity and the rest of a fallen creation.

As well as any human idea can, the idea of love describes God's nature and God's character. Any discussion of holiness as the reflection of that nature and character into the world must revolve around love. Anything we want to call "sanctification," anything that involves becoming like God, is going to look like embodying and displaying the God Who is Love. Holiness and love are inseparable. From a Christian perspective, one could never say, "You can be holy without being loving," or, "That was a loving thing to do, but it didn't look like God at all." In all of our further explorations, we must never lose sight of this central confession of our faith.

There is obviously much more we could say about God, but these ideas are sufficient to move us forward for now. Christians can have a coherent view of holiness because the concept points to the One True God, a God who has a definite nature and character most clearly explained as love. God displays that character through God's good creation by empowering creation to respond to God in God-like ways. And while God's character will always be displayed in action, sabbath reminds us that sanctification is much more about becoming something that reflects God than simply performing a bunch of tasks on God's behalf. These dynamics permeate all of creation, but it is among human beings that God most especially desires to do this work. So, it is to the task of thinking about humanity from the Bible's perspective that we now turn.

Chapter Three

Humanity and the Image of God

God's nature and glory are on display throughout creation, but human beings were created to mirror God in unique ways. We need to understand that in order to understand sanctification. We are tempted to approach holiness as if it is something foreign to human nature, but in fact the very opposite is true. Holiness is humanity's birthright.

When many Christians think about humanity, they start with the idea that human beings are sinners in need of a Savior. In the Wesleyan tradition, however, we try to get behind and underneath that reality. Sin becomes a part of our story and messes up the trajectories that God established for us, but those original trajectories are still important. God did not create us to be sinners. Sin is a malfunction; it is not the way things were supposed to be. God's work of saving sinners is the work of restoring God's original intentions for them, and that is easier to see if we first explore God's holy design for humanity.

Most of Scripture tells us the story of God's dealings with a sinful and broken human race. There are, however, two places where God's primary purposes for us shine through: the stories of creation and the story of Jesus. Genesis reveals what God first created humanity to be. The Gospels show how God became a human being in part to show us what real humanity looks like. We will weave these two testimonies together as we consider this glorious but tragically marred creature that we call a human being.

We will begin with the introduction of humanity into God's story in Genesis 1 and the idea that humans are created in the image of God. From there, we will turn to four testimonies that emerge from the story of unfallen humanity in Genesis 2, testimonies that tell us something of how that image works. First, human beings are composite creatures, composed of earthly dust and divine breath, and their reflection of God is going to be found in—not in spite of—their physical nature. Second, human beings were created as laborers and stewards. They are to be active agents in God's creation who take care of it and further God's creative, order-making agenda. Third, human beings are made to be moral creatures, ones who have real freedom to make decisions about good and evil but only in light of the boundary lines that God draws for them. Fourth and finally, these human beings are communal creatures, created for relationships of equality and interdependence that reflect the loving relationships of God's own Trinitarian nature. Through each testimony, we will explore how it is anchored in Genesis and affirmed by the rest of Scripture, and then we will see how it reaches a renewed anchoring in Jesus.

Image of God

As we noted in the last chapter, God creates most life through intermediaries. In creating human beings, however, God takes a direct hand again.

> Then God said, "Let us make [hu]mankind in our image, in our likeness, so that they may rule over the fish in the sea and the birds in the sky, over the livestock and all the wild animals, and over all the creatures that move along the ground." So God created [hu]mankind in his own image, in the image of God he created them; male and female he created them (Gen 1:26-27).

Images are odd things. There is a famous painting by the Belgian artist René Magritte that portrays the image of an unmistakable smoking device along with a caption above it that says, in French, "This is not a pipe." When it was first painted, the picture left people scratching their heads. "Of course that's a pipe," people would say. "What else could it be?" But the caption speaks the truth. That set of colored strokes of paint on canvas is not a pipe; it is only the image of a pipe. It has no form or weight, no one can smoke it, and a bit of turpentine would destroy it completely. Still, the image fools us for a moment because that's what images do. Images of a thing are not the thing itself, but they remind us of it. They reflect to us something of its nature and character.[1]

That is how the Bible invites us to think of human beings. They are not God. However, when we see how they live and act in the world, they should remind us of God. They point us to God, and the word we use for things that point us toward God is "holy." Being created in the image of God means being created to be holy. Holiness is not something foreign to human nature, some unnatural addition that God imposes on us. It is our birthright, the reason why we were created in the first place.

Though sin will tarnish this image, it is never destroyed. After the flood, murder is prohibited even when killing animals is allowed because human beings bear the image of God (Gen 9:6). Psalm 8 celebrates God's creation of humanity by saying, "You have made them a little lower than God and crowned them with glory and honor. You made them rulers over the works of your hands" (Ps 8:5-6, alt. trans.). The Third Commandment, which prohibits the misuse of God's name (Ex 20:7, Deut 5:11), assumes that human actions reflect back on God. God gets angry at Israel when their activity reflects poorly on God, and God redeems them so that they will do their God-pointing job better (Is 52:5-10, Ez 36:20-28).

In Jesus, we see this image brought into clearest focus. As Paul notes, "The Son is the image of the invisible God" (Col 1:15), and Jesus tells Philip, "The one who has seen me has seen the Father" (Jn 14:9). Jesus goes on to remind the disciples that they are to reflect God through their obedience just as he reflected God through his (Jn 14:10-15). In his Sermon on the Mount, Jesus tells his hearers that their good works are

---

1 The picture is discussed here <https://en.wikipedia.org/wiki/The_Treachery_of_Images> and can also be seen here <https://collections.lacma.org/node/239578>. As Magritte himself noted, "The famous pipe. How people reproached me for it! And yet, could you stuff my pipe? No, it's just a representation, is it not? So if I had written on my picture 'This is a pipe', I'd have been lying!" (Henry Torczyner, *Magritte: Ideas and Images* [New York: Abrams, 1979], 71).

designed to reflect back on God (Matt 5:16), culminating in that striking command, "Be perfect [mature/complete], therefore, as Your Heavenly Father is perfect" (Mt 5:48).

This image of God in humanity, however, is not merely an external reality to be seen by others. Being like God is what makes our personal relationship with God possible. Personal relationships are only possible in the midst of commonalities. We can only relate to that which we are like, and deepening relationships always involve deepening likeness. The same is true of our relationship to God. We were made to be like God so that we could have a relationship with God. Losing our relationship to God through sin impairs the image of God in us, but being restored to relationship with God revives it again. The more like God we become, the more deeply we can relate to God and the more effectively God can relate to the world through us.

If being human means being created in the image of God, then the more like God we become, the more fully we live out our human nature. We often think that we sin because we are human, but that is not true. We sin because we have lost our full humanity, and that is why we can describe sanctification as becoming human again. Like mirrors, we are designed to reflect something beyond ourselves. Cracked or dirty mirrors may draw attention to themselves and not function well as mirrors, but they are mirrors still. They can be cleaned and repaired and restored to function. Despite sin, the image of God still defines us as human beings. As St. John of Kronstadt puts it, "Do not confound man—that image of God—with the wickedness that is in him, because the wickedness is only accidental, his misfortune, sickness, an illusion of the Devil; but his being—the image of God—still remains in him."[2]

Composite Creatures

Beginning with Genesis 2:4, the creation story narrows to focus on God's work with human beings. They are reintroduced into the story as "composite creatures," an odd combination of earthy dust enlivened by the breath of God. Our physical nature and our spiritual, image-of-God nature are designed to work together, and that is part of what makes humanity special.

---

2 St. John of Kronstadt, *My Life in Christ*, trans. E. E. Goulaeff (Jordanville, NY: Holy Trinity Monastery), 310.

Like a potter working with clay, God forms the first human person from the dust of the ground (Gen 2:7). The Hebrew word for "ground" or "earth" is 'adamah, which sounds almost the same as the word for "human person": 'adam, (which some Bibles transliterate as "Adam"). The close association between humanity and the earth is thus embedded in the very words Genesis uses. Humans are earth-creatures. This reminder is important because, as we've already noted, we are easily tempted by the Gnostic illusion that sees the physical as bad and the spiritual as good. We often see ourselves as spiritual beings who are housed—trapped, even—in a physical form. Like scuba divers with artificial breathing tanks, we feel like spiritual creatures forced to live on earth, shackled to these necessary but unnatural physical forms.

Scripture confronts this illusion head on. It presents human beings as earth-creatures, created from—and for—the earth. According to the Bible, humans are physical first and spiritual second; breath is added to dust. Our physical nature anchors the way we bear the image of God. Like an artist who portrays a pipe of clay and wood with paint and canvas, God portrays God's spiritual nature with flesh and bone. God takes a dusty clod, this 'adam made from 'adamah, and breathes into it the "breath of life," and the human becomes a "living being" (Gen 2:7).

Human beings are, then, like a composite of two distinct materials. Sustained by a spiritual life that comes from God, we physical creatures embody the image of a God who is beyond all physicality. The physical processes of chemistry and biology may sustain our cells and organs like those of other animals, but there is more to us than that. We have a "breath of life" that allows us to live in ways that reflect God's Life—at least if we use God's breath the way God intended for us to use it.

The rest of Scripture wrestles with the human condition as physical creatures dependent on a life borrowed from God. When God separates humanity from the Tree of Life in the Garden of Eden, God reminds them, "Dust you are, and to dust you will return" (Gen 3:19). The Psalmist laments this reality (Ps 6 and 90), as does the author of Ecclesiastes (Ecc 12:7). Our physicality makes death our enemy, but even so, there is always hope in God, as Job (Job 19:25-26) and the Psalmist (Ps 49 and 71) both testify.

The enemy of death, however, is conquered in the strongest affirmation of humanity's composite nature: the Incarnation. God becomes a human being "in the flesh" (Jn 1:14) because that is the only way to be human. In Jesus, God takes on tiredness, hunger, and "the thousand natural shocks that flesh is heir to."[3] Jesus reflects the divine nature through—not in spite of—the frailties of flesh. Jesus will die a human death, giving his breath back up to God (Lk 23:46), and God will breathe new life into him in the resurrection. His resurrected body, however, is still a physical one. He eats (Lk 24:41-43), and he can be identified by the flesh-bound scars of his crucifixion (Jn 20:25-27). The rest of the New Testament affirms that our hope for life beyond death is a resurrection like that of Jesus. No other kind of hope makes sense for composite creatures such as ourselves.

This affirmation is important for holiness because God's primary image-bearers are designed to reflect God's character in and through the physical world that God created. Holiness is not an abstract spiritual reality, as though it primarily concerned disembodied souls. While it is utterly dependent on God's spiritual work, sanctification happens in the concrete world we can see, touch, taste, hear, and smell. Even our body with its inconvenient desires and our brain with its awkward chemistry are being sanctified. We look like God when we look like Jesus, and everything Jesus did pointed to God through his flesh.

Laborers and Stewards

When God creates human beings, God gives them some instructions: "Be fruitful and increase in number; fill the earth and subdue it. Rule over the fish in the sea and the birds in the sky and over every living creature that moves on the ground" (Gen 1:28). Humans reproduce like other animals, but they are also charged with living out the image of God in which they were created. They continue God's creative labor by "subduing" and bringing order to the earth, and they steward God's loving rule to all the other living things God made. Right away, Scripture starts filling out what it means to be created in the image of God in terms of creative, care-taking activity.

These affirmations are repeated in Genesis 2. To begin with, there are no plants around before God creates humans, in part because "there was no one to work the ground" (Gen 2:5). However, the first thing God does after making a human is plant a garden. "The LORD God took the man and put him in the Garden of Eden to work it

---

3 William Shakespeare, *Hamlet*, Act 3 Scene 1.

and take care of it" (Gen 2:15). Now the *'adamah* ("ground") has an *'adam* ("human person") to take care of it. Sabbath reminds us that God's image is reflected more in "being" than in "doing," but God is not passive either. God's image-bearers were made to do things; they work in and care for God's creation.

We often paint work in a negative light, seeing it as "toil" and a consequence of the Fall, and many people feel more human on vacation than they do in the office. The Bible, however, paints work in a positive light because it is one of the most important ways God's image shines through us. The word for "work" in Genesis 2:15 is *'abad*, which is usually translated as "serve." It means to do something for the benefit of another or on behalf of another. Human beings exercise God's image by serving God's creation. Serving the garden would have meant carefully cultivating rows and planting seeds, removing rocks and watering the ground. A garden served like that would flourish. In fact, it would become even more productive than a patch of ground allowed to grow naturally. Human creative work is designed to point back to God's creative work, taking a good thing and lovingly making it even better.

In addition to serving the Garden, human beings are supposed to take care of it. That Hebrew word, *shamar*, can also be translated as "keep" or "guard." It means to maintain or to watch over something. Like "serving" (*'abad*), this is activity for the benefit of another, though here it has one further implication. Eden is God's garden; it doesn't belong to humanity. When the man cares for it, he does so as a steward, minding that which he does not own. This makes humanity's service to creation also a service to God. God is, of course, perfectly capable of taking care of the Garden, but God gives human beings a chance to reflect God by giving them a Godlike role in creation, caring for it as God's agents. This is, thus, sanctified work.

Jesus embodies this ideal of active stewardship throughout his life (Lk 2:49, Jn 9:4), and he commissions his disciples to live the same way (Mt 9:35-38, Lk 10:1-3). He also makes it a key point in some of the parables he tells (Mt 25:14-30, Lk 19:11-26). In those parables, servants are entrusted with something that does not belong to them. Their job is to take care of it, but that means making it better. Good servants increase the value of what they were given. Bad servants are not those who lose their deposit but those who fail to improve on it. This reflects the Kingdom of God because God's character is seen through the activities of its citizens.

Moral Creatures

If we think of the "image of God" as the likeness to God that enables us to relate personally to God, one important component of that must be freedom. Personal relationships demand some degree of freedom, and they are impossible under conditions where people are not given any choice in the matter. In the biblical world, this freedom is a gift from God, but it is one contingent upon obedience to God's laws. As moral creatures, we are most free inside of the boundary lines that God establishes for us.

When God made the Garden of Eden, God planted two special trees: The Tree of Life and the Tree of the Knowledge of Good and Evil. Concerning the latter, God tells the human being, "You must not eat from the tree of the knowledge of good and evil, for when you eat from it you will certainly die'" (Gen 2:17). That puzzles us, and we instinctively wonder why God would create such a threat. The Tree of Life we can understand; we are physical creatures subject to death, and our lives are always contingent on God's gifts. But why would God also make a "Tree of Death," as it were? The "knowledge of good and evil" could be a Godlike knowledge of all things or a way to refer to "mature wisdom" (see Is 7:16-15, 1 Kgs 3:9), but it is not a bad thing in and of itself—all that God made is good. Such knowledge is, however, bad for humanity, at least at this point. So God draws a boundary line around the tree and gives the human being something he would not have had otherwise: a choice. God's prohibition against that tree presents those first humans with two alternatives: trusting God's way or going their own.

We instinctively view commandments and laws in a negative light. We think of ourselves as creatures with innate freedom, and so we think of laws as restrictions. Scripture, however, takes the opposite approach. In the Bible, laws create freedom rather than inhibit it because boundary lines are necessary for meaningful choices. God's laws function more like natural laws than human-crafted ones. The law of gravity restricts us to the earth, but it also gives us a freedom of movement we could never have in space. The more we understand the laws of the physical world—laws we cannot change—the more freedom we have in how to use that world to our advantage. In the same way, God's laws tell us how God's created order functions. When we respect those boundary lines, we flourish. When we violate them, things fall apart.

This is why Jesus, like the Psalmist (Ps 19), is so positive about God's law: "Do not think that I have come to abolish the Law or the Prophets; I have not come to abolish them but to fulfill them" (Mt 5:17). Laws against adultery and murder tell us about the things that matter to God. These activities are not bad because God prohibits them. They are bad because they subvert human flourishing, and that's why God prohibits them. Unlike human laws, God's laws are not primarily about the boundary line between guilt or innocence. Instead, they are about the boundary lines between the path that leads to life and the path that leads to death (Deut 30:19). God is free by nature, but human beings are only free by circumstance. Our freedom can only be found on the path that leads to life. As that first man and woman will learn to their sorrow, when we choose the path that leads to death, we drastically cut down on the kinds of choices we can make until there are no choices left to us at all.

In Eden, God uses a good but dangerous tree to teach humans how they are—and are not—like their Creator, and this has implications for how we think about holiness. Reflecting God is only possible within the boundary lines that God draws around that reflection. Holy people pursue some activities because they polish that image-of-God mirror and help them better reflect God into the world. They avoid other activities because they darken or dirty that mirror. As moral creatures, our path to sanctification will always be marked with some signs that say "Do!" and others that say "Do not!"

Communal Creatures

The final testimony we want to hear from Genesis 2 is one that challenges much Western thinking about humanity. In the West, people tend to think of themselves as individuals first and members of a community second. Scripture, however, has other ideas.

When God puts the first human creature in the Garden, we might expect God to offer the typical evaluation for having finished something: "It is good." Instead, we get the exact opposite: "It is not good." More precisely, "The LORD God said, 'It is not good for the man to be alone. I will make a helper suitable for him'" (Gen 2:18). Since we know that God does not make mistakes, we know that "It is not good" means "It is not finished yet." Humanity is incomplete with only one person around. To those raised on the Western ideal of rugged individualism, this may come as a surprise, even though the rest of the world thinks this way naturally. The biblical view of human persons is first of all communal. As the KiSwahili proverb goes, *Mtu ni watu*: "Person is people."

The idea that human beings are communal creatures was already implied in Genesis 1: "In the image of God he created them; male and female he created them" (Gen 1:27). The poetic parallels here place "male and female" next to "image of God," as if the two phrases helped to define each other. If God exists as a Trinitarian community of love, then God's nature can only be reflected by a community. The image of God is not something any of us can develop or display on our own.

This lines up with what we know of human nature from experience. Creatures like lizards or fish can function as good lizards or fish from the moment they hatch. We human beings, however, only mature when we are "humanized" by other human beings. We learn our language and values, our patterns of activity and culture—everything that distinguishes us from the rest of creation—from other people. We are helplessly reliant on other people for a long time before we learn to function on our own. Our much treasured independence is a product of a long apprenticeship of dependence, and that's how God designed us. Our interdependence with other human beings is not a problem to be solved or a weakness to overcome. To the contrary, it creates the best opportunities for us to be as God is and act as God acts, as persons in community who love one another.

Moreover, God signals the kind of communal relationships God wants for all humanity by seeking for that first human being "a helper suitable for him." The Hebrew phrase here is *'ezer kenegdo*, and it can also be translated as "a helper who corresponds to him." The word "helper" (*'ezer*) does not mean "secretary" or "servant" but one who acts alongside of another. Most of the time in the Bible, the word is used to refer to God (Deut 33:29, Pss 121:1-2 and 146:5, Hos 13:9), and God is certainly not Israel's "assistant." The second word implies a face-to-face relationship of equality. This equality is further reinforced when God makes the woman out of the man's rib (connoting a side-by-side connection) rather than from the ground. This makes the woman a continuation of God's creation of humanity rather than something new. When the man meets the woman, he recognizes her without naming her as he did the animals, again showing how they stand on equal footing.

This equality and mutuality is important because human communities are supposed to reflect the Divine Community, and the Trinity has no superior or inferior members. Each human person, like each Divine Person, is different but valued the same. Although power is one of God's important characteristics, human beings do not reflect God well when they take power for themselves over other human beings. Using other people rather than loving them, controlling them rather than serving them, does not make us look like God at all. It is, in fact, one of the hallmarks of sin.

Once again, we see this kind of humanity modeled for us in the Incarnation. Even as the One-and-Only Son of God, Jesus does not work alone. He gathers a community of disciples around him, he empowers them to do the things he does (Mt 10:1, Lk 9:1), and he calls them "friends" rather than servants (Jn 15:15). He also tells them that their discipleship is made most evident in the way they conduct their communal life: "By this everyone will know that you are my disciples, if you love one another" (Jn 13:35).

We humans were created to bear the image of God. Though we are made from dust, we are empowered by God's breath to live a life reminiscent of God's. We are supposed to serve God's creation by being God's agents and stewards, and we have a freedom unmatched in creation so long as we stay within God's boundary lines. Most of all, our communities of mutual dependency and loving interaction are designed to be the places where God's loving and communal nature is most evident. Alas, we human beings thwart God's destiny for us and so introduce into God's reality something that we will call sin, the arch-nemesis of holiness. With that, our story now takes a darker turn.

Chapter Four

The Problem of Sin

At the end of Genesis 2, everything is perfect, at least in the biblical sense of being entirely good and on a smooth track to get even better. We have been introduced to an Almighty God who has brought the world into being. This God works in and through the creation to arrange every good part so that the whole can be pronounced "very good." We have been introduced to creatures made in God's image, human beings. Their vocation is to become physical reflections of God's character as they improve on and take care of this very good world. At this point in the story, there is no hint of evil because everything that exists has been created by God, and everything that God created is good.

Even so, it does not last. Somehow, inexplicably, this entirely good creation is going to fall. All the good-and-getting-better trajectories God has established for creation will go awry, and the creatures made in God's image will reject their God-pointing identity for a miserable substitute they forge for themselves. From that point on, the malfunction that the Bible calls "sin" is going to become the scarlet thread woven into humanity's story. Before we can talk about salvation and sanctification as God's work to restore creation, we need to understand how sin prevents creation from functioning as God intended. This chapter explores that problem.

We'll begin by reflecting on the way the Bible sets up the story of "The Fall," as we usually call it. Sin does not enter the picture as an invasion of some evil thing from outside of God's good creation but rather arises as a corruption of good things within it. We will then walk through the narrative of Genesis 3 to see how that corruption happens and what its consequences are. We will conclude by looking at the layers of the problem of sin in order to better understand how God's salvation and sanctification addresses the problem on every level.

Sin as Corruption

The world that falls in Genesis 3 is one devoid of evil. The tree that occasions the Fall is not an evil tree. There is a serpent whose questions and misleading statements encourage the woman to break God's law, but he, too, is a part of creation. He is not introduced as an evil foreign invader but as one of the wild animals God has made. Even if we identify the serpent with Satan, we still have to say that he, too, started out good and somehow fell. However evil begins, it starts as a corruption from within God's good creation and not as an invasion from without. There is nothing outside of God's creation but God, who is good, and nothing inside creation but the good things God has made.

This means we must be careful with our language about sin and evil. If all the things in creation are good, then evil cannot be a "thing" with substance and location and independent existence. Evil and sin only exist as destructive conditions or malfunctional arrangements between good things. We use the label "evil" for happenings that destroy the good potentials God has built into the world, happenings such as death, disease, or disaster. Under such conditions, the world does not point to the Good God who created it. When human choices and activities foster these destructive happenings, we call it "sin."

Sin and evil are more like shadows than like black marks of paint. A shadow means light has been blocked. We see shadows, and they have an effect on the world, but they do not exist as things we can affect directly. We cannot get rid of a shadow by picking it up or scrubbing it out or burying it under something. We can only dispel shadows by moving the objects that cast them or by shining a new light. Sin and evil function like that. They are absences and holes, not presences and things. In this light, sanctification—the restoration of our capacity to point back to God—is more about rearranging good things and adding to them than about removing evil. We can use metaphors for sin such as cancer, a corrupting malfunction that starts from within and needs to be removed to restore proper health, but those are only metaphors. Sin is not a thing to be removed; it is a shadow that is dispelled when we fill our lives with the light of God's love.

Recognizing that sin and evil exist as conditions between good things also keeps us better on guard against it. If God's perfectly good creation is capable of falling, then any good state of affairs can be corrupted. If we are not careful, we could talk about sanctification as a work of God that frees us up from the possibility of sin and temptation. Alas, even for holy people, there is no such evil-proof state. The first man and woman were perfectly good, and they managed to sin anyway. Jesus was tempted in every way that human beings can be tempted (Heb 4:15), and there was nothing fallen about him at all. Even when all things are good and the world is full of light, there will always be ways of arranging things that cast shadows and block light. In the work of sanctification, God restores the possibility of not sinning but the possibility of sinning is never taken away.

The Story of the Fall

So how do those shadows fall? On some level, sin is irrational and perplexing. There is a "mystery of iniquity," to use traditional language (2 Thes 2:7, KJV), which means there is no "good" explanation for it. However, Genesis 3 helps us with some answers as to why and how God's good creation gets corrupted. Looking at the brief conversation between the serpent and the woman, we see how the road to sin begins with a distorted view of the world. Watching the woman take the fruit and transgress God's boundary line, we see how a distorted view of the world leads to a selfish and distorted set of priorities. Observing the consequences of that transgression, we see how stepping outside of God's boundary lines messes up the relationships that those boundaries were designed to protect. This story helps us better understand our own stories, but it also empowers us to change them. Knowing how the world goes wrong prepares us to cooperate with God's work in setting it right.

In Genesis 3:1, we are introduced to a new character in this story, a serpent who is described as "crafty." Here, again, Genesis is playing with words. The Hebrew word for "crafty" (*'arum*) means being good at uncovering hidden things, and it sounds like the word used to describe the man and the woman as "uncovered" or "naked" in Genesis 2:25 (*'arom*). There is a subtle irony in using nearly the same word to describe both the innocence of humanity and the cleverness of the serpent. While pretending to uncover hidden truth, the serpent will actually hide things and distort the woman's perception of both God and God's world.

The serpent begins by questioning God's prohibition against the Tree of the Knowledge of Good and Evil, exaggerating it to include all the trees of the Garden (Gen 3:1). The implication here is that God has drawn an overly restrictive boundary line for humanity, one designed to inhibit human freedom rather than enhance it. The serpent cannot change the world, but it can change the way the woman sees it. The woman corrects the serpent, but in so doing she also exaggerates God's command, adding a prohibition against touching the tree beyond what God said (Gen 3:2-3, see Gen 2:17). Now it is the woman who portrays God as unreasonably restrictive. It is only a small move in the serpent's direction, but when it comes to sin, small moves matter.

The serpent responds with a crafty set of half-truths: "'You will not certainly die,' the serpent said to the woman. 'For God knows that when you eat from it your eyes will be opened, and you will be like God, knowing good and evil'" (Gen 3:4-5). It is true that the woman and man do not die when they eat the fruit, at least not right away. It is also true that they become "like God, knowing good and evil;" we have that pronouncement from God's own mouth (Gen 3:22). The serpent's statements are true but not in the way the woman expects them to be. Such half-truths conceal more than they reveal. Eating the tree will mean death for them because disobedience separates these composite creatures from the God who is their "breath of life." Given that they were created in God's image, they are already like God. Chasing godlikeness for its own sake will only mess up the godlikeness they already have. The serpent's statements cast a shadow of doubt over God, portraying God as restricting human beings instead of liberating them. This invites the man and the woman to trust in themselves to improve their world instead of trusting God's intentions for them.

The woman then turns her attention to the tree. "When the woman saw that the fruit of the tree was good for food and pleasing to the eye, and also desirable for gaining wisdom, she took some and ate it. She also gave some to her husband, who was with her, and he ate it" (Gen 3:6). Instead of turning to God to restore the trust that the serpent had shaken, the woman looks to tree and thinks about the good things that it offers her. The boundary line that God drew and the good things that boundary line was designed to protect are apparently forgotten or ignored. Her view of reality has been distorted, and it is in acting on that distortion that she sins.

Though evil happens, it is not evil that motivates the woman. In fact, nothing that attracts her to the tree is bad in and of itself. Food is a good and necessary thing for human beings, beauty is a hallmark of God's good world, and Scripture is full of exhortations about the importance of seeking wisdom. As moral creatures, human beings are only motivated by good things, but we can be motivated by the wrong good things. The woman and the man do not fall here because they are looking at God and shaking their fists in spiteful rebellion. They fall because they let lesser goods cast shadows over greater goods. They act toward physical satisfaction and self-promotion and so compromise their relationship with God. They turn their image-of-God mirror away from God, so to speak, and a mirror deprived of light reflects only darkness.

The nature of sin as the antithesis of holiness can be seen in what follows. If the essence of holiness is the reflection of a God of love by creatures created in God's image, sin is the self-absorption that fractures relationships and corrupts that image. Human beings begin to block God's light rather than steward it, and the shadows begin to fall everywhere.

Their new, tree-inspired knowledge opens their eyes, and the man and the woman begin to focus on themselves in a new way. Looking at themselves as if for the first time, they realize that they are naked. Ashamed, they try to hide from each other by covering up with fig leaves (Gen 3:7). This new self-focus, thus, immediately damages their ability to mirror God to and with one another. When God shows up, the fig leaves are not enough, and they hide among the trees. In this act of self-protection, we see that their relationship to their Creator has been broken as well (Gen 3:8). Later, with the curses pronounced on the serpent and on the ground, we see that even humanity's relationship to the rest of God's created order has been disrupted by their sin (Gen 3:14, 17).

God's response to humanity's transgression, however, is surprising. What happens next shows us that this is a story of broken relationships and their redemption much more than a story of broken laws and their punishment. Sin is often depicted as something we human beings do that makes God angry, but that is not what we see in Genesis 3. God does not come thundering into the Garden in wrath to throw lightning bolts and punish the creatures for their defiance. Instead, God knows a shadow has fallen on creation and immediately moves to dispel it. God knows that relationships have been broken, and God's first move is to reach out in reconciliation.

God enters the Garden asking questions. "Where are you?" "Did you eat?" "What did you do?"(Gen 3:9-13). God already knows the answer to these questions, so God is not seeking information. God is trying to start a conversation. The man and the woman are hiding from God, and God's first response is, "Talk to me!" There are, of course, consequences to their disobedience, but not the immediate death that was foretold to them. For both of them, their labor becomes painful, their mutual equality is compromised, and the created order is cursed, becoming resistant to them rather than helpful. Still, it is mercy, not judgment, that gets the last word.

Hiding among the trees of the Garden, the man and the woman are still too ashamed to stand before each other and before God. They cannot fix this situation, but God can. "The LORD God made garments of skin for Adam and his wife and clothed them" (Gen 3:21). The implication here is that God made these garments from an animal, and the only way to get skin from an animal is to kill it. The man and the woman were supposed to die when they ate the fruit, but they did not. Instead, something else dies in order to cover their guilt and their shame and enable them to once again stand before one another and before God. God's first response to sin is not primarily one of anger and judgment but one of mercy and atonement. The story of the gospel is as old as the story of sin. Even the removal of the man and the woman from the garden is portrayed as an act of mercy, albeit a severe one, so that they do not live forever in their fallen state (Gen 3:22-24).

The Image Corrupted

Looking at Genesis 3 through the lenses we acquired from Genesis 2, we see how human beings turn away from the image of God in order to focus on themselves. This self-focus is the essence of sin, and it bends that image-of-God mirror inward so that it reflects nothing but its own emptiness. It is human nature "curved in upon itself," as Martin Luther puts it.[1]

Human beings were created as composite creatures, a physical frame enlivened by the breath of God. The temptation at the tree shows how our focus on physical things leads to an imbalance between our dust and our breath. By seeking to enhance their lives apart from God, they end up radically diminishing it. As Jesus will put it, "whoever wants to save their life will lose it" (Mk 8:35). Restoring our dust-breath balance, then, will be part of restoring the image of God in us.

Humans were made to be laborers and stewards, caring for and improving that which God entrusts to them. Their activity is meant to be directed outward, but in the Fall they focus on themselves. The result, naturally, is the loss of their stewardship, the loss of the Garden. God's sanctifying work in human life is going to restore this outward focus so that human activity once again reflects divine priorities. This does not mean sanctified people do not care for themselves; it simply means that caring for themselves is never their ultimate goal.

As moral creatures, human beings find their freedom within boundary lines. The Fall involves a transgression of those boundaries, and so, unsurprisingly, it entails a loss of freedom. Even Jesus shows us that humanity only points to God by obedience (Jn 14:31, Heb 5:8). Once the humans have lost their freedom, they cannot regain it on their own. Whatever freedom they have must be restored to them by God.

---

1 Martin Luther, *Lectures on Romans* (1515–16), ed. W. Pauk (Louisville, KY: John Knox, 1961), 159.

Sanctification as the restoration of the image of God will set us free, but our freedom can only be exercised within the limits set for it. Otherwise, it, too, can be lost.

It is humanity's communal nature that we see most disrupted in the Fall, and it is that communal nature that God is most interested in recovering. Isolated from each other because of their sin, the man blames the woman and God for his failings and the woman blames the serpent and, by implication, the God who made it (Gen 3:12-13). Their self-focus has not only broken their relationships, it has made them toxic. Outside the garden, it will only get worse, and one of their children will end up killing the other (Gen 4:8). Destructive individuality reflects nothing of God. However, when God restores relationships and empowers human beings to love each other again, nothing reflects God better than redemptive community (1 Jn 3:11-15, see also Ps 133:1).

The story of the Fall is a story of loss. What is lost is that perfect state of creation in which everything reflected well the glory of its Creator. What is lost is holiness in the broadest sense of that term. God, however, does not accept this loss. Despite the fact that the problem of sin is going to get even worse, God does not throw it all away and start over—though God does think about it (Gen 6:5-7). Despite the fact that, as Creator, God can do anything in an instant, God chooses instead to take a longer view and decides to work in and through God's now resistant creation. In dealing with sin, God's give-and-take relationship to creation—especially humanity—is apparently more important to God than getting to the end-goal as quickly and efficiently as possible. Recognizing that is important for understanding how sanctification works.

Sin: Original, Principle, and Act

As Scripture moves on from Genesis 3, we see many ways in which humanity inherits the trajectories of brokenness to which that story testifies. Before we move on to the ways God heals that brokenness, however, we need a quick diagnosis of how the disease of sin functions. Like a disease, sin has three layers. The first is a set of pre-conditions or susceptibilities. This often goes by the name of "original sin," and it helps explain why every single one of us but Jesus ends up falling in the same way that our first parents did. The second layer is the disease itself, sometimes called the "sin principle," the warped condition of our lives that leaves us stuck on ourselves, as it were. The third layer consists of the symptoms of that disease, the acts of sin we commit as we live out our broken condition in the world.

We can think of "original sin" as the brokenness of the situation into which all of us are born. Though we are composite creatures, the physical part of us (our "dust") develops first and is governed by biological impulses toward self-survival and pleasure. We cry for food long before we could ever cry out for God, and we seek out whatever makes us feel good. In time, our "breath" develops and we become more than biological response mechanisms, but by the time that happens, our self-oriented, "me-first" patterns are already well-established and hard to break. Moreover, as communal creatures, we learn the vast majority of those self-oriented patterns from those around us. Alas, all of us were raised by sinners, and so the selfish behaviors of our society, our friends—even our parents and caregivers—all encourage the development of our own selfishness.

Those biological and sociological forces ensure that all of us are accomplished sinners by the time we are aware enough to start making our own choices. Our moral creaturehood, our freedom to make good choices, is compromised even before we begin to exercise it. Like babies born with addictions inherited from mothers who used drugs, we are sick from birth. Aside from Jesus, whose full humanity was never endangered by repeating our first parents' Fall, all the rest of us caught the sin disease because of a compromised immune system, as it were. As Paul notices, "For all have sinned and fall short of the glory of God" (Rom 3:23).[2]

---

2 Some Christian thinkers (like Augustine and many Western theologians after him) also assume that original sin comes along with some original guilt, making us liable to punishment by God even before we commit any sinful acts. This raises some difficult questions, but they need not worry us here. If we assume we are born guilty, we can also assume that the grace of God at work before we do anything is sufficient to atone for any guilt at work before we do anything. As John Wesley notes, God does not condemn anyone on the basis of original sin alone (John Wesley, *Predestination Calmly Considered*, para. 34. See also *Manual*, 28 para.5.2).

We might call this disease that we have caught the "sin principle." Sin is first and foremost a problem of our nature, a corruption of the image of God in which we were created, a malfunctional arrangement of the good things that make us who we are. The condition of sin (mis)shapes everything about us: our motivations, values, attitudes, and activities. It is like a cancer that has metastasized throughout our bodies, and no area of our lives or identities—not even our religion—is left untouched by its ravages. Our sin-condition exists in a feedback loop with our sin-behavior. Our self-focused nature leads us to self-focused actions that make us even more self-focused. In other words, we sin because we are sinners, and we become ever worse sinners as we sin over and over again.

One way to look at our sin-condition is like a behavioral addiction, something that feeds off of our natural brain chemistry instead of an outside chemical like alcohol or heroin. Addicts are those whose brains have been rewired to focus on a particular behavior, sometimes to the exclusion of all else. Our "sin principle" is essentially an addiction to ourselves. We sinners are driven by our concerns, our pleasures, and our well-being over those of everyone else.[3] This self-focus, as we have noted, is the exact opposite of a holiness. Holiness is a reflection of the God of love who voluntarily accepts pain and suffering in pursuit of the good of others. It is this disease, this addiction, this depravity that must be cured and overcome. Only then can we become fully human again: bearing the image of God, reminding others of God, and pointing to God by our actions.

Finally, then, we come to those relationally disruptive acts that we identify as sins. John Wesley famously defined sin "properly" so-called as "a voluntary [or willful] transgression of a known law of God."[4] In other words, acts of sin are those acts of rebellion we commit where we deliberately transgress the boundary lines we know God has drawn. God draws those boundary lines to protect the relationships that God values, and we trample them because we are more concerned with doing good for ourselves than with doing good for other people.

---

3 For a deeper exploration of this metaphor, see Patrick McCormick, *Sin As Addiction* (Mahwah, NJ: Paulist Press, 1989).
4 John Wesley, Sermon 76 "On Perfection", para. II.9 (Bicentennial 3:79).

There are, of course, involuntary acts of disruption, like accidentally stepping on someone's toe. However, we confess and repent of those things without much thought, and we find them relatively easy to ignore and forgive. The small effects of our limited sight or limited understanding do not tend to disrupt our relationships that much—though we cannot afford to ignore them either.

Our rebellious sins, however, are very disruptive. We sinners deliberately stomp on people's toes, as it were, maybe because they cut us off, maybe because we think it would be funny. We actively rebel against God, attempting to thwart God's agenda and God's purposes. These things destroy our relationships, and we cannot repair them simply by saying, "I'm sorry." When we damage and demean and devalue other people instead of serving and loving them, we violate the standard for proper relationship that the Bible calls "justice." Our acts of injustice cannot be shrugged off or ignored, either by us or by God. If there is to be any restoration of relationship after that point, our acts of rebellion must be atoned for.

In this chapter, we have explored how sin and evil are shadowy non-things that impair creation's ability to mirror its Creator. We have also seen how we humans have twisted our God-given, other-centered nature into one that focuses on ourselves. This disrupts our relationships to God, to other people, and even to God's created order. The stage is now finally set for us to explore the marvelous and gracious ways God goes about undoing the damage we have done.

Chapter Five

Salvation as New Creation

As we leave Genesis 3, the world Scripture paints finally looks familiar to us. Loving families and devoted children are placed alongside murderous jealousy and restless wandering (Gen 4:1-12). Civilization and city-building go hand-in-hand with a lust for power and cycles of violence and revenge (Gen 4:17-24). Human beings are blessed with long life, but that life is spent in "painful toil" (Gen 5). People call upon the name of the LORD (Gen 4:26) and then live in ways so opposed to God's purposes for creation that God regrets having included them in it:

> The LORD saw how great the wickedness of the human race had become on the earth, and that every inclination of the thoughts of the human heart was only evil all the time. The LORD regretted that he had made human beings on the earth, and his heart was deeply troubled. So the LORD said, "I will wipe from the face of the earth the human race I have created—and with them the animals, the birds and the creatures that move along the ground—for I regret that I have made them."
> But Noah found favor in the eyes of the LORD. (Gen 6:5-8)

As we saw in Genesis 3, the story of salvation begins in the Garden, when God comes to repair the relationships that the man and the woman have broken. With the Flood, however, we begin to see the story of salvation unfold as a story of new creation. Despite God's entirely negative evaluation of what the world had become—the exact opposite of the "very good" world God had created—God does not follow through with the threat to wipe it out completely. Instead, God decides to "new create" it. Despite the fact that people have become wholly corrupted ("only evil all the time"), God does not give up on the human race. There is one man who finds God's "favor," a word better translated as "grace." God's troubled heart will purge the world of sin, but it will not let sin destroy everything. In graciously saving Noah's family and the animals, God takes the first step toward getting creation back to being what God intended it to be.

In this chapter, we will explore the broad idea of salvation as new creation because it is one of the best ways to understand the connection between salvation and sanctification. It also unites all of God's redemptive work in history, from Genesis to Revelation. God's work to confront and dispel the shadows cast by sin and evil is always the first step in restoring creation's ability to point toward its Creator. God saves in order to sanctify.

Any view of salvation that only affirms what creation is freed *from* without exploring what creation is freed *for* omits half the biblical story of salvation. Christians sometimes limit salvation to the forgiveness for sins or reduce it to the individualistic and spiritual concern of getting to heaven. We rightly rejoice and sing "With my sins forgiven I am bound for heaven,"[1] but those words should celebrate the beginning of God's redeeming work, not the end of it. If salvation is simply forgiveness and heaven, sanctification is unnecessary.

Fortunately, the Bible's presentation of salvation is much broader than that. Salvation in Scripture is a cosmic enterprise involving communities as well as individuals, bodies as well as souls, regeneration as well as forgiveness. It encompasses everything God does to set right what has gone wrong because of sin. We will see that as we explore salvation-as-new-creation in the Old Testament and in Jesus. We will also explore the idea of grace, since nothing happens in creation—old or new—apart from God's initiative. Grace means God always acts first, and God's activity is the foundation for the way creation responds. In that sense, creation, salvation, and sanctification are all works of grace.

---

1 C. Austin Miles, "A New Name in Glory," 1910.

Salvation: Creating Space for Obedience

We have already seen that God is an Empowering Creator. In creation, God acts in ways that invite and empower the response of God's creatures. God's human creatures, however, surrender the freedom God has given them by focusing on themselves. They rebel against God's purposes for creation, and the results are catastrophic. The story of the Flood graphically portrays how sin "un-creates" the world, undoing God's work on the second and third days of creation. The once separated waters come up from the bottom and down from the top and all dry land disappears (compare Gen 1:6-10 with 7:11 & 20).

God's response to this "un-creation," however, is "re-creation," and the story of the Flood is as much about salvation as punishment. God deals with sin because sin is an obstacle to God's purposes, but restoration is always more important to God than retribution. In the Flood, God restores those purposes through Noah, and Genesis articulates this as a work of "favor" or "grace." God saves Noah from the Flood by commanding him to build an ark, making a space that will preserve the potential for both human and animal life after the Flood. Noah responds to this empowering command with obedience (Gen 6:13-22).

There is an interesting connection in the Old Testament between the idea of salvation and the idea of making or creating spaces. One word for "save," *yasha‘*, literally means "to open up a space for" (see Ex 14:30, Deut 33:29, Jdg 2:16, 1 Sam 14:39, Pss 18:3 and 86:2). Likewise, many words for adversity or adversaries are rooted in a word (*tsarar*) that means narrow and restricted (see Num 10:9, Jdg 11:7, 2 Sam 24:14, Ps 6:7 and 129:2). The Hebrew language reflects an intuitive connection that most of us feel. Being "saved" means being "set free," and being free means having space.

The idea of salvation as "opening up a space" also ties salvation and creation together. In creation, God makes the sky as a space between the waters (Gen 1:6-7), God makes space in the sea for dry land (Gen 1:9-10), and God makes a space for humanity by planting the

Garden (Gen 2:8). In fact, the whole creation story can be read as God making an enormous temple-like space in which and through which God can relate to all that is not God. In creation, God makes the spaces that make relationships possible. When sin comes in, it "un-creates" those spaces, constricting and disrupting those relationships. In salvation, God performs a new creation: healing those disruptions, opening up those relational spaces again, and enabling creation to get back on track.[2]

This is not our typical way of looking at salvation, but it highlights the connection between overcoming sin and restoring the potential in creation that sin has compromised. In both a literal and a metaphorical sense, personal relationships require spaces and places in which to develop—homes, businesses, social clubs, even online forums. When we enter new places, we open up the possibility for new relationships. When we form relationships, we "make space" for other people in our lives. When we focus on ourselves, however, we take that space away.

Space is a useful metaphor for thinking about the potential for relationships, but that potential is meaningless unless we activate it. If we do not respond to the possibilities created by our spaces—if we ignore the people in our home or we never greet the new faces we see in the market—then no relationships develop. In salvation, God re-creates the space for relationships that sin has ruined, but that potential is meaningless unless we respond—and that response looks like obedience. As A. W. Tozer notes, "Salvation apart from obedience is unknown in the sacred scriptures."[3]

In Eden, God makes a space for humanity and asks them to respond in trust and obedience. The Fall happens because the man and the woman respond selfishly instead. As a result they lose the Garden, their ideal relational space. In the Flood story, all of humanity loses all of its space because of disobedience. God saves Noah by instructing him to build an ark, but that salvation requires Noah's obedient response. After

---

2 As the Old Testament scholar Terence E. Freitheim puts it, "The objective of God's work in *redemption* is to free people to be what they were *created* to be, the effect of which is named salvation...The redemptive victory of God frees the creation to *become* what God intended" (*God and World in the Old Testament: A Relational Theology of Creation* [Nashville, TN: Abingdon, 2005], 10-12, italics original).

3 A. W. Tozer, *I Call It Heresy: Twelve Timely Themes from First Peter*, (Cabin John, MD: Wildside Press, 2010), 7.

the Flood, God promises a new beginning and commands the humans and the animals to once again "fill the earth" (Gen 9:1, echoing Gen 1:28). Alas, humans again respond with disobedience. They refuse to "fill the earth" and choose instead to gather together and build a tower at Babel so that they can make a name for themselves and not be scattered. God addresses their disobedience by confusing their language and scattering them away, and so even that space is lost (Gen 11:1-9).

In Genesis 12, God chooses Abraham and his family to be the primary representatives and examples of God's saving work. Abraham is not in trouble, but God still "saves" him by offering him a relationship, and that means making a space for him. God promises Abraham a land in which his descendents can dwell securely as recipients and agents of God's blessing (Gen 12:1-8). When those descendents are oppressed in Egypt, God saves them by opening a space in the Red Sea, separating the waters from the waters just as God did in creation (Ex 14:21-22). This salvation, however, still requires an obedient response, and the pattern for that is laid out in the Law at Mt. Sinai. The Law draws boundary lines around the kind of relationships God wants, and Israel is to live in their new space, the "Promised Land," in a way that reflects God's nature and character. In other words, God saves the people of Israel in order to sanctify them.

Israel, however, disobeys. They refuse to trust God and so end up wandering in the desert for forty years (Num 14, 32:13). The space that God opens up in salvation—both the literal space of the Promised Land and the figurative space of relationships—is a conditional space. The Exodus gives Israel the possibility of living in covenant faithfulness to God, but it does not force them to do so. Disobedience amounts to a rejection of God's salvation. That link is further reinforced in the book of Joshua, where obedience opens up the Promised Land for Israel, and in Judges, where disobedience again leads to restriction, oppression, and chaos.

The books of Samuel and Kings tell us how Israel does with its God-given space. Some of its rulers like David (1 Sam 13:14) and Josiah (2 Kgs 23:25) lead Israel to be obedient stewards of the land. Others, like Omri (1 Kgs 16:26) and Ahab (1 Kgs 21:25), lead the people astray. Eventually Israel's self-focus and sin will so corrupt the land that God will take away their space and send them into exile (Lev 18:26-28, Ez 36:18). Even there, though, God saves them. God recreates the nation of Israel (Ez 37), brings them back to the land, and allows them to repair their walls and their temple (Ezra and Nehemiah). With the spaces of their political and religious life restored, Ezra reads them the Law, once again reminding them how they are to respond to God's salvation (Neh 8).

Throughout the Old Testament, salvation is portrayed as new creation, restoring the spaces of right relationship whenever disobedience compromises them. When Israel is oppressed by the sin of others, God saves them. When Israel sins and becomes the oppressor, God judges them. God's concern is always for proper relationships and the laws that maintain them, but this is often depicted, literally and metaphorically, in terms of relational spaces: the Promised Land, the home, the Tabernacle, the wilderness, the Temple, and Zion.

God's salvation, however, is not yet complete. Fixing the problem of sin and self-focus requires more than an external law that outlines how people are supposed to live. Knowing what God wants does not mean we will always do what God wants. As Paul points out, the law ends up being powerless because it was "weakened by the flesh" (Rom 8:3). The self-addiction of our sin is an internal problem that will always keep us from flourishing in the spaces for relationship that God opens up for us. Fallen human beings need more than *in*formation; they need *re*formation. They need to be formed anew, re-created. So, God sends Jesus.

Incarnation: The New Creation of Humanity

When we think about salvation in Christ, we usually focus on the cross, but we will save the important interconnections between salvation, sanctification, and Christ's atoning death for the next chapter. Here, we want to focus on the salvific nature of Christ's life. The story of the Incarnation is the story of God's new creation of humanity. As we noted earlier, human beings were created in God's image so that they could have personal relationships to God and each other as they reflect God's nature and character into the world. In their self-focus and sin, they abandon that trajectory. In the Incarnation, God came as a human being in Jesus to remind us of our true nature and to show us how that nature should be lived out.

For Paul, Jesus is the New Adam, undoing by his obedience the consequence of Adam's disobedience in the Garden (Rom 5:19). Throughout the Gospels, we see Christ modeling and proclaiming God's vision for human beings and their relationships to God and one another. Jesus walks the path of obedient response to God (Jn 5:19, Heb 5:8) and loving response to his neighbor (Mt 9:36, Lk 10:30-37), and he exhorts his followers to walk that path with him (Mk 8:34, Jn 13:15). Jesus not only fulfills the Law as God intended (Mt 5:17), he sharpens it by distilling it down to its essence, which is the law of love (Mt 22:36-40, Rom 13:10).

In so doing, Jesus illustrates those various facets of true humanity we discussed in chapter three. His faithful obedience and response to temptation (Mt 4:1-11, Lk 4:1-13) shows us how we as moral creatures can flourish inside the boundary lines God draws for us. Jesus's approach to adversity, suffering, and death shows us how we embrace the "dust" part of our composite creaturehood without being dominated by it. All of Jesus's miracles and preaching exemplify the labor and stewardship God wants of God's agents in the world. Finally, his sacrificial love and concern for everyone around him shows us communal creatures how we find our true identity in the way we relate to others. Jesus came as a tangible, fleshy, perfect example of what it means to bear the image of God (Col 1:15).

Jesus's example, however, is not enough for us to understand his coming as "Good News." Examples alone do not save us, and we've all seen examples we were powerless to follow. Fortunately, Jesus came to empower us to respond to God, not merely show us how. Incarnation as new creation means that Jesus came to *be* the way, not just demonstrate it.

Jesus empowers us to respond to God with "the holy obedience of love made perfect"[4] by sharing his very life with us. John talks about this as being born again into a new kind of "eternal life" (Jn 3:1-16), and he compares sharing in Christ's life to the way a branch shares in the life of the vine (Jn 14). For Paul, it is by participating in Christ that Christ-followers become new creations themselves (2 Cor 5:17, Rom 8:29, and Col 3:10).

Christ models the movement from old creation to new creation as one that passes through death into life. So, we share in Christ's death so that we might share in Christ's life (Rom 6:3-5), both

---

4 *Manual*, 31.

in a figurative way in baptism and in a real way as we suffer to follow Christ (Rom 8:17, Phil 3:10-11). Second Peter and the book of Hebrews echo this perspective as well (2 Pet 1:4, Heb 12:10).

In Matthew, Mark and Luke, Jesus gives a name to this space of salvation-as-new-creation that God is establishing in him. He calls it "The Kingdom of God" (or "Kingdom of Heaven"), and it shows how he expects his new-created followers to respond to God's salvation. In some ways, the Kingdom of God is like a New Israel. Israel was supposed to reflect its God by how it lived, and citizens of the Kingdom of God reflect the character of their King. In the Old Testament, God had anointed kings and priests as God's representatives, but they did not lead the people in obedience. In the New Testament, it is Jesus, the "Anointed One," the Christ or Messiah, who gathers a new group of twelve around him and leads God's people in faithful response to the salvation-as-new-creation that he himself embodies.

One way that happens is with miracles that demonstrate the "new creation power" of God's Kingdom. Jesus heals the blind and cures the sick and empowers his followers to do the same (Mt 10:1, Lk 10:17, Mk 6:7). These are saving miracles that restore people's freedom, and so it is no surprise that many of them come with instructions: "Show yourself to the priest" (Mt 8:4), "Go and tell (Lk 8:39), "Stop sinning" (Jn 5:14). Being saved means being empowered to respond.

Jesus also leads his followers by proclaiming what the Kingdom of God looks like and pointing out the kinds of responses the Kingdom demands. To serve God as King means repenting (Mt 4:17, Mk 1:15), forgiving (Mt 18:21-35, Lk 17:3-4), seeking (Mt 6:33, 13:44-46), stewarding (Mt 25:14-30, Lk 19:11-27), and having compassion (Lk 10:25-37). Living in the space of God's salvation means reflecting the things that God values. In fact, in many of Jesus's parables of the Kingdom, those who refuse to embody its values are excluded from participating in it, but it is important that we get the sequence right. The Kingdom empowers people to respond; responses do not earn people the Kingdom. It is by failing to respond that people exclude themselves from the Kingdom. God does not preemptively kick them out.

Eventually, we know that Jesus will return to complete the work of "new creation," and God's temple of creation will be fully restored. God will dwell with human beings (Rev 21:3), and we will live a forever-life with God (1 Thes 4:17). The emphasis of Scripture, however, is always on the ongoing work of salvation-as-new-creation here and now. Again, with Paul, "If anyone is in Christ, the new creation has come" (2 Cor 5:17)—not "will come in the future." In Christ, God has restored humanity's freedom (Jn 8:36, Gal 5:1), freedom to live again as agents and reflections of God's own love and grace. Salvation prepares the way for sanctification.

Grace: The Empowering Presence of God

Despite the importance of human response, however, we must never lose sight of the priority of grace. In creation, both old and new, the first move is always God's. Noah, Abraham, Moses, David, Nehemiah, the disciples, Paul—none of them go looking for God. God always finds them first. Whatever human beings do in salvation is an extension of what God has already done. Even when human beings do not respond well to the freedom God creates and re-creates for them, God responds to those failures with unconditional love and second chances. The "free, unmerited favor of God" that we call grace is the bedrock on which the whole edifice of salvation is built.

The biggest error we make when talking about grace is to think of it as a thing, especially if we think of sin that way. If sin is the disease, then grace is the medicine, right? It's the bleach or eraser for the black mark on our hearts. It's the spiritual "stuff" that flows from God when we pray for forgiveness or take communion. We say that we need grace the way we say we need water or air. However, while such word pictures are occasionally helpful, we must not let them mislead us.

As we have seen, sin and evil are more like shadows than like things. They label the conditions and dynamics that take away from the potential for human flourishing rather than enhance it. They represent "spiritual entropy," as it were, the tendency of self-focused activity to always fall apart. If grace is the remedy for sin, then it must be found in the conditions and dynamics that promote human flourishing, particularly as that is found in love. Therefore, we should not think of grace as a "thing" that exists apart from God. Grace labels the condition of God's undeserved goodwill and the dynamic of God's unconditional love and faithfulness. Like holiness, grace is a manifestation of the character of God. While God enjoys responding to the responses of God's creation, God always gets the first word as well as the last one. Throughout Scripture, salvation happens because God shows up and starts putting things right: removing barriers, restoring relationships, creating the freedom to respond. Understanding grace as this active, redemptive presence of God helps us resist any temptation to view salvation as a mechanical or impersonal event. Like "friendship" or "justice," the word "grace" points to a quality of interaction between persons. In salvation, one of those persons is always God.

God wants a relationship with God's creation, and relationships require interaction and response. The kind of responses God wants are always loving ones, but the self-addiction that we call sin makes truly loving responses impossible for us fallen human beings. Our salvation and our new creation, thus, are found in the way God empowers us to respond to God. It is the restoration of full potential much more than the accomplishment of a task. It is the opening and re-opening of a space for relationships. God's grace is that work of God in us that frees us from our addiction to self and so frees us to be able to love others again.

All relationships develop as a combination of two things: decisive moments of commitment and sustained periods of interaction. Grace empowers both of those in our relationship to God. There are critical moments of decision that we experience as crises in our lives, but these punctuate a more gradual relational process that happens over time. What God does only requires a moment, but what we do requires time. The original creation story does not take seven days because God is slow but because God chooses to work in time and to give creation a role in its own development. The same is true with our new creation stories. Grace works by inviting and empowering human response, and God seems content to be patient with that sometimes slow and erratic process (2 Pet 3:9).

Because every person is unique, so is every personal relationship. And yet, every personal relationship has things in common with every other personal relationship. The same is true of our relationships to

God. Every spiritual journey develops differently, and God is never confined to a single pattern of invitation and response. At the same time, there are still typical ways that our relationships to God develop, and it helps us to know them up front. To use another metaphor, since the dance of grace involves both invitation and response, knowing its steps in advance helps us dance more gracefully, so to speak.

We cannot relate to that which we do not know, and God's first overtures toward us are only ever seen in hindsight. So, we experience God's grace first as a "prevenient grace," a grace that comes to us before we go looking for it. God works through the circumstances and people in our lives to bring us to an awareness of God's reality. Whether we were born into Christian homes or come to know God later in life, grace brings us to a point of response where we are given the freedom—unknown to us before that point—to accept or reject God's relational invitations.

We cannot relate to another, however, when we are focused on ourselves. Giving up on our self-addiction and turning to God usually entails a crisis of conversion, a complete reorientation of our lives. However it happens for us, God's saving grace empowers us to repent of our past and allow God to begin healing the mess we have made of our lives. We can now begin to relate to God in a personal way. However, for that relationship to grow, there are two more things that grace must empower.

First, we cannot relate deeply to another person unless we make some kind of commitment to them and to the relationship between us. Our crisis of conversion entails a real commitment to follow God in Christ, but the other commitments that drive our lives do not necessarily disappear. We often struggle with our commitment to God because we try to add it as a new piece into our lives, and that new piece does not always fit well with the other pieces already there. Eventually we realize that our relationship to God requires a total and exclusive commitment. Our relationship to God must become the defining relationship of our lives, the one from which all other relationships flow. If we do not set ourselves apart for God and for God alone, we will always struggle to relate well to God. Some relationships require complete commitment if they are going to progress at all, and our relationship to God is that way. That's the first piece, but commitment by itself is not enough.

Second, we cannot relate to others unless we share something in common with them, and our relationships can only deepen as those commonalities do. Relating to God, therefore, demands that we become like God. Our commitment to God will only sustain itself if we allow the sanctifying dimensions of God's active and redemptive presence in our lives to remake us more and more in God's image. Our attitudes, actions, dreams, and values must all line up more and more with those of God. As we become more like God, our relationship to God matures and our relationships to other people become channels through which God can relate to them as well.

We might compare this dance of grace to the development of a romance. A young lady notices someone, and so she takes steps to get him to notice her as well. Once he knows she exists, he can respond to the invitation to be a friend, and that opens up new possibilities for her as well. As the dance of their friendship deepens, both of them can make steps toward becoming more than friends. These steps, however, require them to orient themselves solely to one another, since some relationships can only develop in the context of exclusive commitment. If the dance goes well, small commitments transform into larger ones. Dating leads to engagement and marriage, and that opens a whole new relational dimension for them. So, moments of encounter lead to processes of development that lead to other decisive moments that lead to new possibilities for development, and that's how romantic love matures and grows.

There is a long history of comparing God's relationship to humanity with a romance because both are relationships built around love. Grace means that God makes the first moves, and we respond. This makes us aware of further moves on God's part, and those moves further empower our response. Through decisions and commitments, our relationship grows deeper. The more we become like God, the deeper we can relate to God and the deeper God can relate to and through us. This is what it means for God's image to be new-created in us by grace.

Chapter Six

Conversion as Initial Sanctification

Having seen the big picture of salvation as new creation, we are ready to understand some of its important details. Through the nation of Israel and the person of Jesus Christ, God has acted decisively in history to free human beings from sin and invite them into an ever-deepening relationship with God and each other. We now turn to the more specific ways in which we experience God's salvation in our individual lives. In this chapter, we will look at our conversion as the initial sanctifying event of our salvation, focusing on what happens when we first accept God's offer of redemption and reconciliation in Christ. This will lay the groundwork for discussing the "full salvation" of entire sanctification in the next chapter. There we will focus on the commitments and transformations that anchor the renewal of God's image in us—a renewal that also makes us more effective agents in God's project of new creation. To use our relational analogy again, this chapter is about the beginning of our "romance" with God. The next chapter explores what it means to "marry" God for real.

As we approach these realities, we want to keep in mind that our descriptions of God's work are crafted for our benefit. They never bind God. Human language is limited when talking about God, and God's holiness means that God is always beyond us. Even when the God-Beyond-us comes to be God-With-Us, we never fully comprehend God's work. We explain it with metaphors and analogies, but we never capture or control it with our words. Through the lenses of Scripture, we can identify God's work and say in faith, "God did this!" But that is very different from saying, "God must do this!" Seeing how God has worked in the past gives us confidence to trust how God will work in the future, but it never ties God's hands. God is always free to do new things (Is 43:19, Hab 1:5), and God is never confined to the pictures we paint so that we can make sense of God's work. The artist does not get to tell the flower how it must grow; she only tries to express its beauty. Likewise, God's followers point to God's work; they do not dictate God's activity.

When it comes to the beginning of our salvation, the Bible gives us many beautiful word pictures to help us understand how God forgives sins and gives us new life, but none of them are perfect descriptions of the process. For Christians, salvation is anchored in the death and resurrection of Christ, and Scripture presents that work as a sacrifice (Jn 1:29, Heb 10:10), as a ransom (Mt 20:28, 1 Tim 2:5-6), as a punishment (Rom 3:25-26, 1 Pet 2:24), and as a victory (Col 2:15, Heb 2:14). All of those images are truthful, but none of them contains the whole truth. Since God's grace is about empowering us to respond, we know that God gives us enough understanding of salvation to accept it and live accordingly, but that is all. There will always be something mysterious about Christ's life and atoning death, and that is a good thing. The goal is perfect obedience, not perfect understanding (see Jas 2:17-19).

As we saw in the last chapter, the work of grace starts in prevenient ways that bring us to an awareness of God, and this awareness makes us want to repent and turn back to God. Grace empowers our response, and we usually identify some initial, decisive moment of turning back to God as our conversion, our "salvation experience." What happens at that point is portrayed in Scripture with many metaphors, but we will content ourselves with four of them: life and the metaphor of new birth, death and the metaphor of sacrifice, family and the metaphor of adoption, and innocence and the metaphor of justification. In each case, we will explore how these word pictures help us to understand our conversion as our initial sanctification. Our turning to God sets us apart for God, who becomes the exclusive object of our devotion, but it also empowers us to reflect God's nature and character to the world. We will also see how each metaphor naturally invites us to think about what comes next.[1]

"You Must Be Born Again": Regeneration and Initial Sanctification

In the Gospel of John, Jesus confronts the Jewish leader Nicodemus with a statement that has him scratching his head. "Jesus replied, 'Very truly I tell you, no one can see the kingdom of God unless they are born again'" (Jn 3:3). Entering the new creation space that Jesus calls "the Kingdom of God" is about living a completely different kind of life, and nothing evokes "new life" like the image of a new birth. Perhaps that is why the idea of being "born again" has become the most common way for evangelical Christians to describe their conversion experiences. Where our sin had once bound us to a path that led only to death, we are now free to follow a path that leads to everlasting life.

The Christian idea of "rebirth," however, is different from the Buddhist or Hindu idea of reincarnation. There, rebirth is a literal matter; one is actually born again in a new body and in a new place and time. Christian rebirth is metaphorical, which is why Nicodemus struggles to understand it at first. When we come to God—or rather, when we accept God's coming to us—God's Spirit breathes into us a new kind of life, an "eternal life" (Jn 3:16). This is a life that reflects the life of God, which makes it by definition a holy life. That new life, however, is still attached to the same biological life we have lived since birth. As

---

1 For a deeper and fuller exploration of the work of atonement and salvation, see Eric M. Vail, *Atonement and Salvation: The Extravagance of God's Love* (Kansas City, MO: Beacon Hill Press, 2016).

Jesus tells Nicodemus, the biological (water and flesh) and spiritual are both a part of the Kingdom of God (Jn 3:5-6).[2] Our lives have been derailed from God's original purpose because we turned inwardly to focus on ourselves. God restores the kind of life that God intended for us all along—a life lived for loving relationship to God and others. This is why we sometimes use the idea of "regeneration" to talk about the new birth. It is the word we use when something grows back—a lizard's tail, for instance, or a starfish's arm—after it has been lost.

Given the strong link between sin and death throughout the Scriptures, it comes as no surprise that salvation from sin means being restored to life. When Moses finishes recounting the Law to the people of Israel, he offers them a choice between an obedient life oriented on God or a disobedient return to captivity and destruction (Deut 30). Proverbs 10:16 lays out the same options: righteous life or wicked death. Even when Israel ends up in exile because they focus on themselves, God still offers them a new birth (Is 66:7-11). God gives Ezekiel a graphic vision of this rebirth and regeneration (Ez 37) by restoring life to a valley of dry bones that represents the nation of Israel.

Coming to the New Testament, the idea of new birth and new life is anchored most strongly in Jesus's own resurrection. Jesus's death, like his baptism, demonstrates God's full identification with a fallen and broken humanity whose end is always the grave. When God raises Jesus, however, God charts a new course for humanity out of death and into a new and deeper life. This new life is a life dedicated to and empowered by God, and that makes it a life that God can use to further God's Kingdom. This is, therefore, a sanctified life, one that reflects God's nature and character. As Paul puts it, "God made him who had no sin to be sin for us, so that in him we might become the righteousness of God" (2 Cor 5:21). Sin is always connected to death, but righteousness is connected to new life.

---

2 The NIV translation is misleading. In John 3:6, the dynamics of water and spirit are joined by "and," not "but," in the original Greek text. No contrast or opposition between the two is implied.

As Jesus's baptism and death demonstrate his identification with us, so our baptism demonstrates our identification with him, both with his death and with his new life. As Paul puts it, "We were therefore buried with him through baptism into death in order that, just as Christ was raised from the dead through the glory of the Father, we too may live a new life" (Rom 6:4, see also Col 2:12 and Tit 3:5). Because Christ promises to raise his followers from the dead one day (Jn 6:40), we know that this new life is one over which death has no real hold (1 Pet 1:23).

The Bible uses "new birth" to talk about new beginnings. Our stories do not end with our birth; they are only getting started. It makes little sense to see the moment of our conversion as the pinnacle of God's work in us. Being born again or being regenerated is important because of the new life that it makes possible. Our new birth is a decisive and irreplaceable step in our relationship to God, but it is far and away not the final step on our journey. We talk about it so that we can talk about what comes next.

"Abba, Father": Adoption and Initial Sanctification

Like all births, our birth into this new life is a birth into a new family. That brings us to the second metaphor we use to describe conversion as initial sanctification: adoption. The idea behind adoption is that someone who is not biologically connected to a family is nevertheless made a full member of that family. This can be a formal and official matter in which this new relationship is recognized by law, or it can be an informal matter of treating someone so much like family that the lack of shared DNA makes no difference. Either way, the idea covers all those cases where family transcends blood relationships and becomes a matter of voluntary love rather than biological accident.

Adoption is, thus, a good metaphor for God's familial relationship to God's people. God's nature transcends biology, and so God is not a "father" in any literal sense of that word. Nevertheless, God has chosen to commit Godself to human beings so strongly and care for them so completely that God ends up being more "father-like" than any earthly, biological father could ever be. God adopted Israel as his "treasured possession" and wanted them to understand themselves as God's children (Deut 14:1-2). When the prophets articulate God's frustration with Israel's disobedience, it sounds like a father with an errant child (Jer 3:19 & 31:20, Hos 1:10 & 11:1-9).

In the New Testament, Jesus is shown to be God's Son in a way more real than the language of adoption can cover. In John's language, he is the "unique" or "only-begotten" son (Jn 1:14,18 & 3:16,18), a son "by nature," as it were. However, part of Jesus's mission was to extend the recognition of God's fatherhood to everyone who would receive him and his message. Such people are given the right to become children of God (Jn 1:12). Trust in Jesus leads to our adoption into God's family, and all of this flows from God's love (1 Jn 3:1). Paul, too, picks up on this theme, affirming that it is by the power of the Spirit (Rom 8:14-17) and by faith in Christ (Gal 3:26-29) that we confirm the familial relationship that God had always wanted for us (Eph 1:4-5).

God makes Godself part of the human family in Jesus so that, through Jesus, human beings can become part of the family of God. Again, Jesus demonstrates his complete identification with us through his life, his baptism, and his death. God then demonstrates God's commitment to overcome human death by raising Jesus to life. Our acceptance of these realities leads us "back home," as it were, much like a Prodigal Son (Lk 15:11-32). Our conversion experience is that moment when we finally put away our rebellion and self-focus and return to the Father God who has been loving us all along. Our baptism represents our entry into this new family. Jesus becomes like our elder brother, and all the rest of God's adopted children become our brothers and sisters. Our love for each other then reflects the love that is God's very nature. In the words of Hebrews: "Both the one who makes people holy and those who are made holy are of the same family. So Jesus is not ashamed to call them brothers and sisters" (2:11). In this way, our adoption is our initial sanctification.

Like all adoptions, however, our adoption into God's family is a beginning, not an ending. Having been "set apart" as a member of God's family, we are now empowered to become more like God, to develop those "family resemblances," so to speak. We all share the imprint of the family in which we grew up because of everything we learned from them. We don't need our father's DNA to pick up his hand gestures or love of cooking nor our mother's genes to pick up her tone of voice or her passion for baseball. Family resemblances happen because families form us over time, and the family of God works the same way. We had to give up our self-focus and rebellion in order to enter into this family, but that only gets us started. Living in this family means loving and serving, growing and helping others to grow, even when we disagree. Adoption is an invitation to family, but that is a reality that must be lived out to be meaningful.

"The Lamb of God": Sacrificial Atonement and Initial Sanctification

John the Baptist introduces Jesus to the crowd around him by saying, "Look, the Lamb of God, who takes away the sin of the world!" (Jn 1:29). In John's Jewish context, the idea of a lamb who takes away sin would have immediately evoked the idea of sacrifice in everyone's mind. Christians have always understood Jesus's death as a sacrificial death, and our trust in Christ entails an appropriation of that sacrifice. However, we often misunderstand how sacrifices work, and that leads us to misinterpret the idea of Christ as our sacrifice.

In the polytheistic and pagan world surrounding Israel, sacrifices were the way one gave earthly goods to the heavenly gods. These goods were usually livestock, and one offered them to the gods to either appease their anger or cultivate their favor. The right sacrifices performed in the right way would, in theory, make the gods relent from whatever disaster they were using to punish the people or make them look in favor on the people when they went to war with their enemies. In either case, these sacrifices were designed to influence divine behavior much the way that giving gifts to important people might get them to use their influence to benefit the gift-giver.

While Israel's sacrifices looked similar on the outside to those pagan sacrifices, they were driven by a completely different understanding of God. The first stories of sacrifices from people like Cain and Abel (Gen 4:3-5), Noah (Gen 8:15-20), Abraham (Gen 22:1-14), and Jacob (Gen 45:25-46:1) all show that they make offerings to God in response to what God had already done—not to get God to do anything. After all,

66

the God that Israel serves is a God of grace, and that means God always makes the first move. Many of Israel's "food offerings" (e.g., Lev 2-3, 7) function the same way, as acts of recognition and thankfulness in response to God. Sacrifices give Israel an embodied language of gratitude, not a way for them to manipulate God.

Sacrifices also serve as an embodied language of sanctification or consecration. After the Exodus, God claims ownership of every firstborn male in Israel (Ex 13:1-16). This ownership is publicly recognized by giving back to God sacrifices that recall the tenth plague God sent on Egypt. Animals (aside from donkeys) are given directly back to God by being killed, but Israel's God wants no child sacrifices. Instead, the children are redeemed, "bought back," from God by a substitutionary sacrifice that still recognizes them as rightfully God's.

Finally, sacrifices are used as a language of cleansing and atonement. This is the function of the sacrifices on the great Day of Atonement described in Leviticus 16. The Most Holy Place and that altar were supposed to be holy, set apart for God. However, Israel's sin taints those sacred realities, and so they need to be cleansed in order to be seen as holy again (Lev 16:16, 19). The people, too, have rebelled and turned away from their role as a holy people who display God's nature and character to the world. They, too, need to be cleansed and brought back into their proper relationship with God so that they, too, can serve God's holy purposes again.

It is against this background of gratitude, sanctification, and atonement that the New Testament talks about Jesus as a sacrifice. Jesus is the substitute lamb that allows us to be recognized as God's without having to die to prove it. Jesus's blood is the "cleansing agent" for rebellion and sin that allows God's people to be made holy again. These are, naturally, metaphors. Sin is not a thing that can be literally washed away by a substance like blood. Instead, blood represents the death that is the inevitable consequence of rebelling against the Author of Life, and so blood makes the consequences of sin repulsively visible. John uses this idea to refer to Jesus as our "atoning sacrifice" (1 Jn 2:2, 4:10), and Paul compares Jesus to the "mercy seat," the physical place where blood was applied to atone for the sins of the people (Rom 3:25). The author of Hebrews portrays Jesus as both priest and sacrifice, one who offers himself once and for all to make atonement for all sins (Heb 9, also 2:17).

In Christ, God has acted to save us from our sin and restore our broken relationship with God. We respond to this work not by making new sacrifices of our own but by accepting the one God has already made on our behalf. Once again, it is in our baptism that we identify with Jesus's death (Rom 6:3), and that identifies us with his sacrifice. This makes our initial experience of salvation in Christ the first moment of our sanctification. Like Israel, we have turned away from God, and in so doing we have defiled or profaned our lives. Like Israel, we need to be cleansed and sanctified so that our lives are once again devoted to God and God's purposes.

This atonement, however, has to be lived out. A sacrifice can only represent the restored relationship between God and God's people; it is not enough to make sure sin does not happen again. For that, the people had to respond obediently and live in holy ways that reflected the way God lived. Of course, the people would not do that, and so a new sacrifice had to be offered every year. With Jesus, however, it is supposed to be different. His once-for-all sacrifice is designed to introduce us to a life that is exclusively dedicated to holy obedience, and yet many who accept Christ find themselves struggling just as Israel did. This suggests that something more than sacrifice is necessary to empower the kind of "sanctified life" that God desires.

"The Gift of Righteousness": Justification and Initial Sanctification

One final way we can understand our experience of conversion is with the entwined metaphors of law, guilt, and punishment. Salvation entails justification. God does not hold our offenses against us, and we are saved from the punishment due to us for violating God's laws.

"Sin is lawlessness," John reminds us (1 Jn 3:4), and when we sin and focus on ourselves, we always transgress the boundary lines God established. God's laws are designed to protect our value as human beings and to safeguard our proper relationships with God and one another. In other words, these laws show us what God means by "justice." When we selfishly trample the boundary lines God has established for our good and our freedom, we dishonor

God and we devalue ourselves and one another. Whether or not we feel guilty for such wrong actions, they make us guilty. They place us firmly inside the "blast radius" of God's wrath whenever God decides to finally make things right. The apostle Paul puts it this way:

> But because of your stubbornness and your unrepentant heart, you are storing up wrath against yourself for the day of God's wrath, when his righteous judgment will be revealed. God "will repay each person according to what they have done"
> [Ps 62:12]. To those who by persistence in doing good seek glory, honor and immortality, he will give eternal life. But for those who are self-seeking and who reject the truth and follow evil, there will be wrath and anger. (Rom 2:5-8)

Before coming to Christ, we were "children of wrath" (Eph 2:3, NRSV). However, when we allow God to make us God's children—giving us a new birth and adopting us into God's family—we also receive forgiveness for all that. In that sense, we are "justified" or declared "not guilty" and given the "gift of righteousness" (Rom 5:17), the grace of being made "right" with God.[3]

It is important to note that Christ's death on the cross is not what causes God to forgive us. God has always intended to forgive, which is why God sent Jesus in the first place. However, to forgive others for their offenses is not the same thing as pretending there are no consequences to their actions. God expresses this paradox to Moses when God's glory passes by him on Sinai (Ex 34:5-9), and God demonstrates it to Israel by forgiving their rebellion but still letting them suffer for their poor choices (Num 14, esp. 20-23). When we are justified, God's forgiveness makes our relationship with God "right." It does not, however, pretend that nothing happened. In fact, unless we recognize the weight of our offenses and the degree to which we have messed up our relationships, we cannot put them right. This is why forgiveness and repentance go hand-in-hand in the Scripture.

This perspective helps us see why the cross is so important for our justification. God does not have to punish sin; God is God, and that means God does not *have* to do anything. However, God does not want us to think that our forgiveness means that our law-breaking

---

3   In the world of the New Testament, the word we translate "righteousness" (δικαιοσυνη) is built from the verb "to justify" (δικαιοω), so the two concepts overlap much more in the biblical languages than they do in English.

does not matter. Normally, we punish people for breaking laws, and that punishment represents the value of whatever it is that the law was designed to protect. The penalty for parking illegally is a small fine, but the penalty for killing someone is life in prison, and the difference in punishment represents the difference in value between other people's inconvenience and their very life.

God's laws are designed to protect the things God values: people and loving relationships. God will not to say to us, "I declare you not guilty" without also recognizing the pain and suffering our sin has caused to other people. That would be the same as saying to those we have hurt, "Your pain does not matter." Those people matter very much to God, and that's why God's anger burns against those who are "self-seeking" and "follow evil." Seen as the punishment for sin, the cross represents both forgiveness and justice, God's solidarity with us sinners but also God's solidarity with the victims of our sin.

See from one side, the cross demonstrates how seriously God takes sin by showing us what the punishment for sin looks like. In that sense it is like a father who voluntarily burns his finger with a match to show his children why they should not play with matches. When we recognize that our sin "burns" both us and other people, we want to turn away from it. By taking the "wrath-full" consequences of our selfishness on himself, Jesus reflects back to us the ugliness of our sin. If that does not make us want to turn away from our sins and dedicate ourselves completely to God, then no other argument God could offer would either. As we repent, we see that God has forgiven us and "canceled the charge of our legal indebtedness, which stood against us and condemned us; he has taken it away, nailing it to the cross" (Col 2:14).

In this way, our justification becomes our initial sanctification. We symbolize this in our baptism, which is both our testimony that we have turned away from our sins (Acts 2:38) and God's testimony that God has forgiven us for them and washed us clean (1 Pet 3:21). Like prisoners released from their cells, we are freed from the guilt of our sin so that we can dedicate our lives to the one who set us free. We can turn away from our self-centeredness only because God has turned us toward God-centeredness. As Paul puts it, "You have been set free from sin and have become slaves to righteousness" (Rom 6:18). The work of God that justifies us also puts us on the path to sanctification.

Which brings us to the other side of the cross, the side that shows Christ taking the place of the victims of sin as well as the victimizers. On the cross, Christ suffers alongside everyone else who suffers when we twist the world so that it serves us. Christ's voluntary and innocent suffering points to something about God. It is "sanctified suffering," suffering that displays the loving character of God. The pagan centurion next to Jesus's cross sees this (Mt 27:52, Mk 15:39) as well as one of those crucified with him (Lk 23:41). This is the side of the cross that Peter exhorts his readers to emulate (1 Pet 2:21-22 & 4:1). The cross that Jesus carries to make us right with God is the same cross he invites his followers to carry as they follow him (Mt 16:24). Christians are not called upon to suffer again for their own sins; they are called to suffer innocently so that other people can see in them the same God they see in Jesus. Justification is, thus, an initial sanctification, setting us apart for God's service and helping the rest of the world see God for who God truly is.

Each of the metaphors we have explored conveys the idea that our experience of conversion is only a beginning. New birth and adoption open up for us the chance to live in new ways in a new family. Because we are consecrated to God and cleansed by Jesus's sacrifice, we are called to live in ways that ensure that this sacrifice was not in vain. In the same way, being justified and set free from the punishment of sin invites us to follow a path that does not lead us back into sin's prison and so make our initial release from it meaningless. So how does that happen? What more can God do than adopt and rebirth and redeem and justify us? God can sanctify us entirely, and it is to that work we can now finally turn.

Chapter Seven

Entire Sanctification

We finally come to the heart of the matter. Everything we have explored up to this point—the nature of God and humanity, the problem of sin, and the work of salvation—has been designed to help us understand the work of God we call "entire sanctification." For John Wesley, the doctrine of entire sanctification, or "full sanctification" as he sometimes called it, was "the grand depositum which God has lodged with the people called Methodists; and for the sake of propagating this chiefly He appeared to have raised us up."[1] Since Wesley's time, Methodist churches, Holiness churches, and others who have inherited his movement have continued to claim that the pursuit of holiness is the hallmark of Christian life and that there is a distinctive experience that anchors us in this pursuit.

Using our romance analogy, we could say that God is not content with a "dating relationship" with God's people. It is not enough that they enjoy having God on their side and like to spend time with God but basically still do their own thing. God wants a "marriage," a complete and exclusive commitment from God's people that mirrors the

---

1 John Wesley, "Letter to Robert Carr Brackenbury," Sept. 15, 1790, *The Letters of the Rev. John Wesley, A.M.*, ed. John Telford, 8 vols. (London: Epworth, 1931), 8:238.

commitment God has to them. God wants a people completely set apart for God, totally devoted to reflecting God's nature and character in the world, fully engaged as God's agents in the world—in other words, entirely sanctified.

We'll begin by discussing the problem of "partial conversion," which explains why we must hold out God's call to be "entirely converted" or entirely sanctified. There is a difference between being turned toward God and living a life that reflects and embodies God's nature, and God's people have wrestled with that gap throughout Scripture. We will then explain why that gap so often exists, which explains why a further work of God beyond conversion is often necessary—especially for those whose conversion did not represent a radical reorientation of one's life. Finally, we will explore what this further work of God looks like: what sanctification is and what's so "entire" about it. We will also see how Jesus models this sanctified life for us in a way that allows us to equate sanctification with Christlikeness.

More Than "Converted"

Everywhere we look in Scripture, we see that God's redeeming work expects a redeemed response. Abraham is instructed to walk before God "faithfully and be blameless" (Gen 17:1). God's saving work in the Exodus is immediately followed by God's instructions at Mount Sinai on how to live a "saved life." This includes the Levitical refrain "Be holy because I, the LORD your God, am holy" (Lev 19:2, also Lev 11:44-45, 20:26, 21:8). Israel's flourishing as a nation is tied to obeying God's commandments. From Nathan (2 Sam 12) and Elijah (1 Kgs 18:15-40) to Isaiah and Malachi, God's prophets are always confronting disobedience and encouraging proper responses to God. Jesus understood his own life and ministry as an obedient response to God (Jn 8:25-29), and he cast discipleship in the same terms. Paul understood this, and his first letter finishes with exhortations like, "It is God's will that you should be sanctified... For God did not call us to be impure, but to live a holy life" (1 Thes 4:3-7). The call to holy living is the culmination of Paul's exploration of the gospel in Romans (Rom 6-8), and even the last echoes of Paul's voice in the New

Testament include the recognition that God "has saved us and called us to a holy life" (2 Tim 1:9). James (Jas 2:24) and Peter (2 Pet 3:11) say similar things. It is impossible to read the Scripture with attention and avoid the call for God's people to live in ways that reflect God.

However, it is also impossible to read Scripture without seeing that God's people often dodge that call—not always, of course, but often enough for us to notice. The gap between God's call and our response is not a necessary one, but it shows up with uncomfortable frequency. Abraham lies out of fear and self-protection (Gen 12:10-20), and one of the first things Israel does after God saves them is make an idol and offer sacrifices to it (Ex 32). Judah's good kings are always tearing down idols (e.g. 1 Chron 14:12, 2 Kgs 10:26-28 & 22:4-20), but that does not seem to help. The very existence of the prophets and the fact that Israel preserved their writings proves that Israel struggled to fully devote itself to God. They worshipped idols (Is 2:8, Jer 2:11, Ez 23:49) and followed their own selfish agendas (Am 8:3-7, Mic 2:1-3). Even the coming of Christ does not solve this divided loyalty. Before Jesus's death and resurrection, the disciples suffer from the same bickerings and betrayals that Israel did (Mk 9:33-37 & 14:50). Pentecost secures those disciples-now-apostles in their devotion to Christ, but not everyone who was converted in the early church followed as obediently—as the story of Ananias and Sapphira shows (Acts 5:1-11). All of Paul's letters were written to Christian communities, but some of these communities suffered from some grievous sins (1 Cor 5:1, Gal 1:6). The book of Revelation begins with a long series of similar accusations (Rev 1-3). So, even in Scripture we see that not everyone who claims to follow Christ follows him fully.

How do we explain this? We could say that such "partial followers" are not actually saved at all and so have no faith to live out. We could say that salvation is an "all or nothing" reality, and if one does not have it all, one has nothing.[2] That view, however, does not seem to fit either Scripture or Christian experience. After all, Paul and the Revelator are

---

2   This was the major debate between John Wesley and the Moravians who helped him find his own assurance of faith. He discusses the various degrees of faith in his sermons "On Faith" (Sermon 106) and "On the Discoveries of Faith" (Sermon 110).

writing to Christian communities, and their warnings and instructions make little sense to non-believers. Alternatively, we could say that partial conversion is "normal." We could say that all God's exhortations to holiness are empty and that it is actually impossible for God's earthly followers to follow God's heavenly program. There are many Christians who feel this way, but one cannot hold this view without ignoring much of the Bible, as we have seen. A better explanation is to say that there are people who have been saved and have begun their journey with God but who have not yet discovered the kind of discipleship that exclusively devotes itself to God's agenda and displays God's nature and character to the world.

Given that biblical salvation is more about the restoration of a relationship than the accomplishment of a task, this comes as no surprise. God can accomplish tasks instantaneously, but relationships take time. God's saving work puts us on the path to heaven, but there is a journey that gets there. God's forgiveness restores our relationship to God, but relationships must be lived out. If the problem of sin were nothing more than a violation of law, then it could be dealt with by some combination of punishment and pardon. However, if sin describes the way our self-orientation causes us to ignore God's boundary lines and disrupt our relationships to God and other people, then we cannot fix that problem without completely reorienting our lives. Our relationships are not automatically repaired just because some punishment has been meted out or withheld. God can punish or forgive all the individual sins God wants, but if we are not empowered by grace to respond to that discipline or forgiveness with a desire to love God and love others, then we are still under sin's power. To be truly free from sin's grip, we need more than a mere turning toward God. We need to be entirely sanctified.

Untwisting our Nature

In order to understand entire sanctification, we need to understand why followers of God and disciples of Jesus so often struggle to live out their faith. God wants to turn us away from a self-focused path that leads to death toward a God-focused path that leads to life, and yet we frequently drag our feet. Why? Because we have been so corrupted and compromised by sin that we no longer want what is good for us. We have twisted the image of God in us into an image of ourselves that is threatened by God's call to holiness. On top of that, our self-focus has created so many layers of malfunction—from ignorance to selfish acts to a self-absorbed nature that actually wants those things—that we seldom notice the deeper layers until we deal with the superficial ones. Our unfolding salvation is a bit like fixing a car that won't run, not realizing that the transmission needs to be overhauled until after the starter has been fixed. Fortunately for us, God's grace is strong enough to fix whatever problems sin creates. As Paul puts it, "Where sin increased, grace increased all the more" (Rom 5:20).

As we have seen throughout this exploration, human beings were created in God's image so that they could have loving relationships with God and each other. This image is crafted to be a tangible, visible reflection of our intangible, invisible God, and it also empowers us to be God's creative agents in the world. A necessary part of that image is the capacity for free choices because loving relationships cannot be created by compulsion. Alas, we human beings have used the freedom and creativity God gave us to serve ourselves rather than God. In so doing, we have not only broken our relationships, we have turned inward and corrupted our relationships into means for selfish ends rather than ends in and of themselves. The result is that our very identity has been warped. This is why God's grace has a bigger job than forgiving and accepting us; God must radically reshape us. We need more than salvation from God's wrath; we need to be saved from ourselves.

Entire sanctification is about that part of salvation. It is about fully living out our conversion. The first stages of God's new-creative work in our lives empower us to turn toward God, and that should never be depreciated. However, when we are reborn, adopted, atoned for, and justified, we enter into our new life with a lot old and ingrained patterns of self-oriented living. They have become a part of who we are, forged by the decisions and commitments we made before we accepted God's salvation. God could, of course, instantly give us a new set of desires and values and activities—reprogram our brains, as it were—but those "new people" would not be "us." In fact, we would probably not even recognize them. This is why God does not instantly change us to match

God's ideal for us. God loved the real "us"—broken sinners that we were—not the perfect vision of us God has in God's mind, and love does not force change. Instead, God invites us along a path of new decisions and commitments that allow us to respond to that vision without violating our personhood. The God who gave us freedom to become sinners now empowers in us a greater freedom to become saints. It simply takes time.

Free from "The Law of Death"

Paul gives us one vision of how this works as he unpacks the implications of the gospel for the Romans. He uses the idea of the law to show how our knowledge of God's boundary lines does not automatically make us want to follow them. In fact, to self-oriented sinners, it does the opposite. It makes us want to rebel, even though we are converted enough to know in our heads that rebellion is wrong. In other words,

> For I have the desire to do what is good, but I cannot carry it out. For I do not do the good I want to do, but the evil I do not want to do—this I keep on doing. Now if I do what I do not want to do, it is no longer I who do it, but it is sin living in me that does it. So I find this law at work: Although I want to do good, evil is right there with me. For in my inner being I delight in God's law; but I see another law at work in me, waging war against the law of my mind and making me a prisoner of the law of sin at work within me. What a wretched man I am! Who will rescue me from this body that is subject to death? Thanks be to God, who delivers me through Jesus Christ our Lord! (Rom 7:18b-25a)

When we come to God, we want to want what God wants. That change of heart is part of our initial sanctification, but those new godly desires have some competition. We want loving relationships with God and others, but we want other things, too. Paul here takes the voice of one who struggles between what he *knows* is good and what he *feels* is good. The struggle is a sign that grace is at work, but it is still a struggle. Freeing ourselves from ourselves is a challenge, and God often makes things possible without making them easy. Fortunately, the battle is one we were destined to win.

We struggle because we come to God with long-standing habits of self-orientation that we acquired during the time we spent running away from God. Some of these habits are rooted in our physical biology, driven by our needs for food or security or by our desire to seek pleasure and avoid pain. Others are rooted in social desires, driven by our need to connect to other people and receive their approval. All of them are facets of the condition we have called "original sin," and these self-oriented desires do not tend to disappear when we come to Christ. Our God-directed and self-directed sets of desires usually live side-by-side in our lives—at least at first. James diagnoses this conflict of wills as the source of problems in the church (Jas 4:1-10), and Paul reminds the Galatians, "For the flesh desires what is contrary to the Spirit, and the Spirit what is contrary to the flesh. They are in conflict with each other, so that you are not to do whatever you want" (Gal 5:17).

This clash of desires, however, is not "just the way it is." God wants more for us than a perpetually divided life. As Paul affirms in Romans 7:25, we are delivered from this "wretched" condition by Christ. He then goes on to explain how this happens:

> So then, I myself in my mind am a slave to God's law, but in my [flesh] a slave to the law of sin. Therefore, there is now no condemnation for those who are in Christ Jesus, because through Christ Jesus the law of the Spirit who gives life has set you free from the law of sin and death. For what the law was powerless to do because it was weakened by the flesh, God did by sending his own Son in the likeness of sinful flesh to be a sin offering. And so he condemned sin in the flesh, in order that the righteous requirement of the law might be fully met in us, who do not live according to the flesh but according to the Spirit. (Rom 7:25b-8:4, *alt. trans.*)

Paul articulates the cause of our divided life as a tension between two "laws," two sets of boundary lines or patterns for living. One of them is rooted in our self-serving physicality—our flesh. The other is rooted in God's life-giving Spirit. What mere words on a page could not do, God's Spirit in Christ accomplishes, setting us free from the power of our flesh so that we might live the way God has called us to live.

We can illustrate the dynamic Paul describes by looking at the way physical forces interact to make an airplane fly. The law of the flesh is like the law of gravity, the constant force pulling the airplane down toward the earth. Airplanes, however, can fly because there is also another law at work on them. Technically called "Bernoulli's Principle," that law describes how faster moving air has less pressure than slower moving air. As long as the airplane is moving fast enough, the shape of the wing allows the faster moving air on top of the wing to pull the airplane up. The laws of fluid dynamics set the airplane free from the law of gravity. The law of gravity does not disappear, of course, but its force is overcome by stronger forces at work.

According to Paul, a similar thing happens in our spiritual lives. The bio-chemical impulses of our brain and body are always pulling our decisions toward self-preservation and self-orientation. That is the "law" of our flesh or our "members," and it is the law to which we are held captive by original sin. The saving work of Christ, however, breaks the power of that law by introducing a new dynamic into our lives: the law of the Spirit of life. By grace, God helps us see that our selfish desires are not good—either for us or for anyone else. Sin creates the illusion that we can be our best selves by focusing on ourselves, but God knows that our best selves are found in loving relationships with God and others. This is why our sanctification is often described as being made perfect in love. When God fully captures our attention, God empowers us to take our attention off of ourselves and devote it others. This is why sanctification must be seen as a work of grace, a work that God empowers in us but one that we could never accomplish on our own. The idea that we could free ourselves from ourselves by ourselves is nonsense. The idea, however, that God wants to fully free us from ourselves so that we can fully be ourselves sounds like good news.

God does this by establishing a new pattern, a new law, for our lives. This law is oriented toward love and life rather than self and death. So long as we obey this new law, the other law does not keep us down. Of course, like gravity, that other law never goes away. As long as we are alive, we will feel our biological and psychological impulses just like the airplane is always subject to the law of gravity. The point, however, is that those impulses are no longer in charge. They are constantly overcome by forces far stronger than they. The battles are still there, but they are battles we always win because it is God who is fighting them.

This is how God frees us from the conditions of "original sin"—not so much by eradicating them or suppressing them but by overwhelming them. By relying on God's work in our lives, we are freed from the domination of our physical desires. We can say "No" to ourselves and "Yes" to others, devoting ourselves to their good rather than our own and thereby reflecting God's loving nature. By finding our anchor in God's love for us, we are freed from the need to please others. We need no longer seek their approval or fear their disapproval because we are no longer focused on ourselves. We are free to love regardless of how other people respond. Naturally, the temptation to follow our fleshly desires or our social situations never goes away—even Jesus had to wrestle with that (Mt 4:1-11, Lk 4:1-13). However, a life that, like Christ's, is entirely devoted to God is not attracted to earthly things with the same power that it is attracted to God and what God wants. We may not want pleasure or approval any less, but we do want God so much more.

This analogy between our spiritual lives and that airplane also helps us to see why this new life takes time to develop. Getting our "spiritual engines" started at the moment of our salvation does not get us instantly into the air. It takes most of us some time and struggle to reorient our lives toward perfect love, to reach the "spiritual speed" we need for our obedience to the Spirit's prompting to become our new way of life. However, if we keep going, there will come a moment when God empowers a kind of "spiritual take-off," a moment when we experience the reality that "the law of the Spirit who gives life has set you free from the law of sin and death" (Rom 8:2). There is a moment when our sin-twisted nature finally untangles enough for us to fully devote ourselves to God. With a pure heart focused on God and God alone, we can begin to fly, begin to live and love as God created us to. We call that moment "entire sanctification."

Recovery from Self-Addiction

Another helpful analogy to our recovery from self-focus is found in one of the metaphors we used earlier for sin: addiction. Addictions represent the pinnacle of our self-serving biology, twisting our personhood and identity to revolve around a chemical or a behavior. Addicts become so attached to their addiction that they do not care what relationships they break or who they hurt. Addictions make people miserable, and they drag everyone around them into that misery as well. Earlier we described our "sin principle" as an addiction to ourselves, a corruption of our nature that makes us self-absorbed and relationally disruptive instead of self-sacrificing and loving. We can use the analogy between sin and addiction to help us to understand why sanctification is a necessary component of a Christian life.

Suppose a small group of people befriends a lady named Mary, and Mary is a drug addict. Mary has little room in her life for friends because her world revolves around her addiction, but this group decides to be her friends anyway. Sadly, Mary owes her drug dealer a lot of money, and the dealer is threatening her. If these friends are particularly resourceful and devoted to Mary, they might scrape up enough money to pay off the drug dealer and keep Mary safe. However, while paying off her addiction-driven debt would be a great blessing, Mary is still an addict. Her new friends still have a hard time relating to her, and before long she owes her drug dealer a lot of money again. That cycle could go on until her friends run out of resources or simply give up, but there is another option. If they really want to help Mary and be her friends, they need to do more than pay off her debt. They need to encourage Mary to get into rehab so that she can be free from the addiction that is destroying her life and keeping her in debt.

Now, rehab for Mary is not likely to mean that all desire for her chosen drug goes away. Given the way many drugs reshape the brain, most addicts find that they always have some desire to light up or shoot up or take that drink. This is why attendees at recovery meetings introduce themselves by saying, "Hi, I'm Joe, and I *am* an alcoholic," rather than saying, "I *used to be* an alcoholic." Recovery from addiction is usually possible only when people keep their weakness to their addiction firmly in front of them. Of course, the goal of rehab is to give people the networks and tools and help they need to overcome the desires that keep them in cycles of addiction. So, Mary will likely always need those friends to help her stay clean, but they can hope for that day when Mary has taken her last hit and the battle against her addiction becomes a cycle of victorious living rather than a cycle of regular defeat.

In many ways, sanctification is like rehab for the self-addiction we call sin. Entire sanctification represents that moment when our wrestling match with our self-orientation becomes a consistently victorious one instead of one in which we always get pinned. The idea of a victorious struggle might not seem appealing at first, but it is much better than the alternative. Addictions give their sufferers only occasional moments of rest against a constant background of pressure and failure, and sin works the same way. Rehab helps turn that dynamic around so that the struggles become the occasional realities and stability the constant one. Entire sanctification represents the same fundamental shift in the life of a sinner. Someone at a recovery meeting might stand proudly and say, "I'm an alcoholic, but I've been sober for twenty years," and everyone would clap for the ongoing victory that represents. So, too, followers of Christ can testify and confess, "I am a sinner, but by the grace of God I've been so focused on loving my Savior and other people that I cannot remember the last time I deliberately turned my back on them."

The analogies of both a "spiritual take-off" and a freedom from addiction also help us see another important truth. Entire sanctification is not so much a once-and-done event as it is the start of a new way of living. It is the entry into a life of perfect love, but that is still a life we live in our bodies with all their fleshly impulses. Therefore, it is always possible for us to turn our backs on the grace that keeps us "airborne," the grace that keeps us "clean," and return to our old flesh-driven way of life. Of course, why would we want to land once we learned how to fly? Having tasted freedom from our self-addiction, why would we want to return to those chains? It would be crazy, but it is nevertheless possible. This is why the sanctified life requires cultivation, attention, even confession. It is a set of relationships to be nurtured much more than a task that God has accomplished.

Seeing how original sin has twisted and corrupted our nature helps us to see why something more than mere conversion is necessary, why "full salvation" must go beyond forgiveness for our sins. Living truly "saved" lives that reflect the God who saved us requires a decisive victory over sin, one that goes beyond merely preventing sinful actions. We now turn to the way we discover this decisive victory—this "spiritual take-off," this freedom from self-addiction—in our lives.

Becoming Human Again

Even though it can be a struggle, we should remind ourselves that sanctification is something quite ordinary for human beings. We were created in God's image, and so it is natural for us to reflect our Creator. God's image in us is what enables us to relate to God and to one another because God's nature is love. Sanctification is the recovery of that image, being made perfect in love, and so it is more a matter of personal relationships than impersonal tasks. This is why the analogy of marriage works so well to articulate the commitments and transformations that allow us to live lives completely devoted to God. Fleshing out that analogy in more detail gives us a good sense of how entire sanctification unfolds.

In Western dating relationships, couples move from a general but exclusive orientation toward each other into a lifelong set of commitments that involve joint bank accounts, a shared living space, and often the decades-long mutual project of raising other human beings. There is no rule about how long the "practice commitment" takes before the "real commitment" takes over, but the transition point between the two is traditionally a big public ceremony called a wedding. Weddings are decisive events, but they happen because there was a lot of gradual growth before them, and they set up a new kind of growth that takes place after. They serve as a "graduation ceremony of love," so to speak, the culmination of one kind of relationship and the "commencement" of a deeper one.

The decisive event that we label "entire sanctification" functions in a similar manner. We begin our relationship to God with our conversion and initial sanctification. God introduces us to God's ways and invites us to walk in them, but too often our way still gets in the way. We struggle because we want to follow God but we also try to do things our way. When we cooperate with God's love, we become more loving and look more like God. When we rely on our own efforts, we constantly trip over ourselves and end up doing selfish things rather than loving ones.

We are committed to God, but we find ourselves also committed to other things. We want God, but we also want security. We want to please God, but we still want to please ourselves. We want God's plan for our lives, but we want it to fit in with the plans we have already made. It is those other commitments that we must surrender. We cannot become like God, reflect God's image to the world, and serve as God's agents in the world by playing the "God and…" game. Those things only happen when we play the "God only" game, and that demands a complete and unreserved commitment.

How does that happen? From one angle, it looks like an act of entire consecration. "Consecrate" is the word we use in English when human beings set something apart exclusively for God. Our entire consecration means that we agree to "marry" God. We give God our unconditional obedience and allegiance, and we bind our time and talents and energies and bank accounts and living spaces—everything about us—to God and God's purposes. To use Paul's image, we fully surrender to the "law of the Spirit who gives life" (Rom 8:2). To use our addiction metaphor, we check ourselves into "self rehab." It is a decision we make, a commitment we offer. That usually feels like a big deal to us, and most people remember that moment as a decisive event in their spiritual lives.

From another angle, however, the commitment we make is actually God's work of entire sanctification. God is an empowering creator who works in and through creation to enable it to respond properly to God. The reason we can decide to consecrate ourselves to God is that God has already empowered us to overcome our selfishness and enabled us to make that commitment. We do not act so that God can respond. Our commitment is our response to what God has already done. We consecrate ourselves because God is sanctifying us; God does not sanctify us because we consecrate ourselves. Paul puts it this way: "Continue to work out your salvation with fear and trembling, for it is God who works in you to will and to act in order to fulfill his good purpose" (Phil 2:12b-13).

This unreserved commitment to God is the mark of a mature relationship to God, which is why we also refer to it as "Christian perfection." We have outgrown our selfish spiritual "toddlerhood." We are finally back on track to becoming what God had originally created us to become: fully human, image-of-God persons empowered by the Holy Spirit to live as Christ would live in our particular situation. We have let God perfect us in love and free us from fear (1 Jn 4:18) so that our actions reflect God's loving character and our work is directed at God's loving ends. In his most famous work on the subject, *A Plain Account of Christian Perfection*, John Wesley explains it this way:

> In one view, it [Christian perfection] is purity of intention, dedicating all the life to God. It is the giving God all our heart; it is one desire and design ruling all our tempers. It is the devoting, not a part, but all our soul, body, and substance to God. In an other view, it is all the mind which was in Christ, enabling us to walk as Christ walked. It is the circumcision of the heart from all filthiness, all inward as well as outward pollution. It is a renewal of the heart in the whole image of God, the full likeness of Him that created it. In yet another, it is the loving God with all our heart, and our neighbour as ourselves.[3]

Most of our misunderstandings about entire sanctification are the result of removing it from this framework of personal dedication, devotion, and love. It is not an achievement or a task; it is God empowering us to relate as God does. It is not about making us "more worthy" of heaven; it is about becoming better agents for God on earth. It is not a matter of adding "good works" to our salvation by faith; it is fully embodying our faith-as-trust in God. Trust in relationships is only real where it is acted out (Jas 2:20-26). Relationships are always matters of mutual interaction and response, and it makes no sense to say we have a relationship with someone apart from the way we act and respond to them. Since God wants real relationships with us, we know that requires real responses, however much we acknowledge that such responses are still the product of God's grace.

Looking at entire sanctification through this relational lens also helps us see beyond any artificial distinction between sanctification as an instantaneous event and sanctification as a gradual process. Relationships always contain moments of decision and crisis interspersed between periods of gradual growth. Our human friendships depend on both noteworthy events like the first time we met and on ordinary times of sustained interaction, light conversations, and

---

3 John Wesley, *A Plain Account of Christian Perfection*, §27 (Jackson 11:444).

being together. Relational growth invites critical decisions that open up new possibilities of growth that encourage new decisions and so on and so forth. Both are essential to authentic personal relationships, and that is why we find both woven seamlessly together in our relationship to God.

Finally, focusing on the idea of entire sanctification as a relational commitment analogous to marriage helps us to see what is so "entire" about it. If sanctification referred to the task of removing all the bad things in our lives, we could take the phrase "entirely sanctified" to mean something like "entirely purified." Our growth would be finished, and there would be nothing more to do. However, the idea of "finishing" a relationship makes no sense. Removing the obstacles to relationship is important, but it is only a first step. If, however, we hear the phrase "entirely sanctified" like we hear the phrase "entirely married," we'd be tempted to think it redundant. Is there any way to be married without being "entirely married"? Is there any other way to be faithful than to be "entirely faithful"? Marriage only exists as an entire and complete binding of our lives and trajectories to those of another, and even the things that happen beforehand take their significance from that reality. Likewise, there is no way for us to relate deeply to God and function as God's agent in the world unless we are entirely about the business of becoming more and more like God, entirely about the business of being sanctified. This is also why we only talk about "entire sanctification" and never "entire holiness." The point is to be fully engaged, not to be fully finished. That will not happen until Christ returns and God finishes the work of new creation.[4]

Sanctification as Christlikeness

Even with a good analogy like marriage, the idea behind entire sanctification can be a bit abstract. We can agree with Wesley that we want our hearts "circumcised from all filthiness" and we want "one

---

4   The Church of the Nazarene's *Manual* statement on "Entire Sanctification" is explicit about this. The process of sanctification encompasses initial sanctification, entire sanctification, and "the continued perfecting work of the Holy Spirit culminating in glorification" (31). The process of sanctification, then, cannot be viewed as "complete" with "entire sanctification" because there is more "perfecting" that happens after that point.

design ruling all our tempers" and still have little idea what that actually means. This is why Wesley points to Jesus as our model. It is, after all, "Christ"-ian perfection that we are talking about, perfection in a Christ-like mode. The pattern for the kind of maturity and "full personhood" that God desires for humanity is found in the God-man Jesus.

In Christ, God's perfect love was made incarnate and God's Image perfectly portrayed, perfectly embodied. His every act and every word flowed from God, served God's agenda, and produced a reflection that pointed people back to God. In Christ, God has provided the power and the pattern for renewing God's image in us, and that renewal is what frees us from the sin-scarred image we crafted for ourselves. As we saw throughout chapter three, Jesus helps us to see what true humanity—sanctified humanity—looks like.

Because of sin, our composite creaturehood was compromised, and the desires of our flesh and dust smothered God's life-giving breath. In Jesus, we see how God can be seen in and through our physical form. We see this in his victory over fleshly temptation (Mt 4:1-11, Lk 4:1-13) but also in the way he valued and validated other people's embodied life, healing many and even raising some from the dead (Mk 5:35-43, Jn 11:40-44). We also see it in the way that John articulated the characteristics of repentance in Jesus's coming Kingdom as caring about the material conditions of people's lives, asking the rich to share their abundance and the powerful not to abuse their power (Lk 3:10-14). Entire sanctification as Christlikeness means embodying God's presence in this physical world, concerned about everything that makes up our material life and orienting that life toward the eternal life of the Kingdom of God.

Because of sin, our activity consists of serving ourselves rather than laboring as God's stewards. In Jesus, we get a glimpse of a life entirely devoted to God's service. Jesus himself says that he only speaks what the Father gives him to say (Jn 12:49) and does what the Father commands him to do (Jn 14:31). Jesus understands his own life in terms of sanctified stewardship and mission, and he invites his followers into the same pattern of living (Jn 17:17-19). Entire sanctification as Christlikeness means being a completely devoted channel through which God can work to accomplish what God desires.

Because of sin, we disregard the boundary lines that God draws for human good. In so doing, we compromise our moral creaturehood and lose our freedom to the addiction of sin. In Jesus, we see the exact opposite dynamic. Because he cared so much about proper relationship with God and others, he celebrated the God-drawn boundary lines that protect them and challenged the human-drawn lines that impair them (Mt 5:17-20 & 23:1-28). Jesus did not fulfill God's law as an end in itself. He demonstrated the idea that "Love is the fulfillment of the law" (Rom 13:10), distilling all the commandments down to loving God and loving others (Mt 22:37-40). He modeled for us what the "holy obedience of love made perfect"[5] looks like. He also showed how a life oriented to God was free from all fear, all impulses to self-protection, because "Perfect love drives out fear" (1 Jn 4:18). Entire sanctification as Christlikeness means showing the world how perfect love leads to both perfect obedience and perfect freedom.

Finally, because of sin, we break the very relationships that make us who we are, undermining our communal creaturehood. In Jesus, we see God becoming a part of the human community so that the human community can participate in the divine community that is the Trinity. While Jesus cherishes his times alone with God, those times flow into and out of the time he spends with others (Mk 1:35-39). He gathers a community of disciples and tells them that their identification with him is wrapped up in the way they live in community (Jn 13:35). Because God is love, God's image can only be expressed by love. Our love for God and our love for our neighbor are intertwined expressions of our communal creaturehood that cannot be pulled apart. As Mother Teresa put it, "The important thing is not how much we accomplish, but how much love we put into our deeds every day. That is the measure of our love for God."[6] Entire sanctification as Christlikeness means recovering our relational nature in a way that makes everyone else long for the kind of relationships to God and others they see in us.

---

5 *Manual*, 31.

6 Mother Teresa, *One Heart Full of Love*, ed. Jose Luis Gonzalez-Balado (Glasgow: Collins, 1989), 26.

88

Looking at Jesus and then looking at ourselves, our response could easily be one of despair, and that would be appropriate on some level. There is simply no way we could live like that on our own. "Impossible!" we might say, and we would be correct. Based on human effort and limitation, reflecting God as Christ did is unimaginable. Which is why sanctification must be something more than a work constrained by human limitation and human effort. As Jesus himself notes, "With man this is impossible, but with God all things are possible" (Mt 19:26).

From start to finish, sanctification is a work that God must do. It is a work we can allow or impede, but it is never anything we can accomplish. We do not begin to live and feel differently because we have convinced ourselves that something is true. We live and feel differently because God has changed something about us. God changes our relationship to God in a way that changes our relationships to others and to God's world. Only God is holy, and so only God can sanctify. But because God is holy, God does sanctify. In fact, it is *the* thing that God most desires to do.

However, even though the work is God's, God does not do this work alone. Our Empowering Creator works to recreate us by empowering others to help us in that process. While nothing can replace the individual relationship we have with God, that relationship does not exist in a vacuum. We cannot be recreated as composite creatures in a disembodied way; we cannot be recreated as communal creatures without a community. Our "flight school," our "rehab center," our school for learning to live as Jesus lived (1 Jn 2:6) is the church.

Chapter Eight

The Church: A Sanctified, Sanctifying Community

Sanctification is about recovering God's image in us, and entire sanctification is being entirely committed to that recovery. Becoming more like God opens up new possibilities for our relationship to God, but it also allows us to relate to others and to the world in Godlike ways. Because the ideas of sanctification and the image of God are relational ideas, it makes no sense to talk about them in individualistic terms. As John Wesley famously noted, "The gospel of Christ knows no religion, but social; no holiness but social holiness."[1] Sanctification happens in community, and God's primary earthly agent for that work is the sanctified and sanctifying community that we call "the church."

---

1 John Wesley, "Preface" to *Hymns and Sacred Poems* (1739) ¶5 (Jackson 14:321).

In looking at sanctification as Christlikeness, we hinted at how Christ's pattern for a "new created" humanity restores all the facets of God's image in us. We will now explore that in greater detail. In this chapter, we will discuss the church as one way God restores to us our communal creaturehood. In the next chapter, we will explore how entire sanctification affects our composite creaturehood, our role as laboring stewards, and our moral creaturehood. We will examine the church from three angles. First, we will look at the idea of the "baptism of the Holy Spirit," and how that phrase unites the individual and communal facets of God's sanctifying work. Second, we will look at how two key features of the church's life—worship and sacraments—flow into and out of God's sanctifying work. Finally, we will look at how this sanctified community understands its role as a sanctifying and missional community, corporately involved in God's mission in the world as the Body of Christ.

Baptism of the Holy Spirit

The best place to see the connection between entire sanctification and the church is with the idea of the "baptism of the Holy Spirit." John the Baptist and Jesus both use that phrase to point forward to the event of Pentecost, and the Holiness tradition has often used it to refer to the experience or crisis moment of entire sanctification. For some, this dual use of the phrase has created confusion or tension between the communal and individual facets of the Holy Spirit's work of setting people apart for God. However, if we understand sanctification as the recovery of God's communal image in us, those tensions largely disappear. For individual human beings to reflect God's nature of love, they need a community. Identifying entire sanctification and the baptism of the Holy Spirit helps us to articulate what that means.

When John the Baptist is preparing the people for the coming of Christ, he tells them, "I baptize you with water for repentance. But after me comes one who is more powerful than I, whose sandals I am not worthy to carry. He will baptize you with the Holy Spirit and fire" (Mt 3:11, see also Mk 1:8 & Lk 3:16). John's baptism is a testimony of repentance, but John seems to understand that people need more than a desire to turn their life around. They need to be empowered to live this turned-around life. In that way, John's prophecy echoes the prophecies of Isaiah (44:3), Joel (2:28-29), and Ezekiel (36:26-27) in which God, the Empowering Creator, promises to breathe new life into God's struggling people. Only with God's help can people live in loving community the way God has always envisioned for them.

Jesus picks up on this image after his death and resurrection in order to point his disciples toward the deepening work that God will accomplish among them after Jesus physically departs:

> On one occasion, while he was eating with them, he gave them this command: "Do not leave Jerusalem, but wait for the gift my Father promised, which you have heard me speak about. For John baptized with water, but in a few days you will be baptized with the Holy Spirit." (Acts 1:4-5)

That work happens less than two weeks later, and Acts describes it explicitly as a baptism with the Holy Spirit and with fire:

> When the day of Pentecost came, they were all together in one place. Suddenly a sound like the blowing of a violent wind came from heaven and filled the whole house where they were sitting. They saw what seemed to be tongues of fire that separated and came to rest on each of them. All of them were filled with the Holy Spirit and began to speak in other tongues as the Spirit enabled them. (Acts 2:1-4)

The idea that the Holy Spirit is God's "breath," that which empowers God's people to do God's work, goes back to the Old Testament. God's breath makes the first human alive in God's image (Gen 2:7), and God's Spirit inspires the craftsmen who will build the Temple (Ex 31:2-4, 35:30-32). It empowers the elders who help Moses in the wilderness (Num 11:17, 25-29) and the judges who lead Israel in the Promised Land (Jdg 3:10, 6:34, 11:29, 14:6), and it is through God's Spirit that the prophets are inspired to speak God's words (Num 24:1-3, Is 61:1, Ez 37:1, Mic 3:8). These incidents of the Spirit's activity, however, are individual and episodic. God comes to empower a task, but this empowerment does not seem to be available at all times to all people. The baptism of the Holy Spirit at Pentecost changes that.

As the crowds gather, wondering what is going on in Jerusalem that Pentecost morning, Peter explains to them that this is the fulfillment of Joel's prophecy:

> In the last days, God says, I will pour out my Spirit on all people. Your sons and daughters will prophesy, your young men will see visions, your old men will dream dreams. Even on my servants, both men and women, I will pour out my Spirit in those days, and they will prophesy. (Acts 2:17-18, Joel 2:28-29)

Joel foretells a corporate event, a communal outpouring of God's Spirit, and that is what Pentecost fulfills. Working across lines of age and gender, the Spirit inspires and empowers God's people to see the things that God is doing and testify about them. Unlike God's work with isolated individuals in the Old Testament, this new work of the Spirit creates a new community: the church. As the rest of Acts testifies, the work of the church is the work of the Holy Spirit in the church. In fact, nearly half of all the references to the Holy Spirit in the New Testament are found in Acts. As believers are filled with the Spirit and baptized by the Spirit, they are empowered to do God's work, to show the world what the God of Jesus Christ is like, and to invite others into the same work. Together, by the Holy Spirit, believers become a sanctified and sanctifying community.

This communal dimension of God's image in us then grounds its individual expression, and this is true for both our spiritual and our physical lives. The communal aspect of sanctification forms the background against which God entirely sanctifies individuals. When Paul writes to the church, he consistently calls its members "holy people" or "saints," even when he is chastising some members of the community for their unholy behavior (see 1 Cor 1:1 & 11). The Holy Spirit works to create a holy people (1 Pet 2:5-10), not merely a collection of holy individuals, and the fruit of the Spirit's work is a set of attitudes and orientations toward others (Gal 5:22-25). Paul uses the same marriage analogies that we have been using to describe our complete devotement to God, but he uses it as a way to talk about the relationship between Christ and his church, not God and God's individual devotees (Eph 5:25-33). Everyone shares in this devoted relationship to God together, even while there are some for whom the reality of this devotion pervades their lives more than others.

The "baptism of the Holy Spirit," thus, is not either a personal spiritual transformation or the communal event that gives birth to the church. It can only be understood as both together; separately, the ideas do not make sense. The reality of church is expressed in the lives of its individual members, but individual members only encounter God because there is a "community of encounter" that gave them that opportunity. When we embrace God's sanctifying work with our full consecration, we participate in the ongoing reality of Pentecost. We become a part of the church when we accept God's offer of relational restoration in salvation, our initial sanctification, and the Holy Spirit begins working on us right away. We should not think that God withholds the Spirit until we are entirely sanctified because there would be no way for us to grow toward Christian perfection without the Spirit's active and ongoing presence. However, there is a difference between surrendering to the Spirit's presence in our lives and surrendering to the Spirit's full control. There is a difference between being *in* the church and *being* the church, the holy people of God who make God known to the world. The first, however, naturally leads to the second as God uses our participation in God's holy community to foster and deepen our own recovery of God's image.

Church as Sanctifying Community

Using the analogies we developed earlier, we pointed to the church as our "flight school" and our "rehab center." It is the place where we learn how to cooperate with the law of the Spirit that sets us free from the law of sin and death and the place where we learn to live above our addiction to sin and self. The idea of the baptism of the Holy Spirit shows how hard it is to distinguish between the acts of God that save us and sanctify us and the acts of God that bring us into the church and set us apart as the Body of Christ in and for the world. The church is, thus, a sanctifying community of those being sanctified, and it accomplishes this work through the various engagements and encounters that we call "'worship.'"

The English word "worship" is a contraction of "worth-ship," the acknowledgement of worth, worthiness, or value. In English Bibles, it is used most often to translate words for "bowing down" and "serving," which are the two primary ways in which ancient cultures recognized superior "worth." As the work of the church, worship includes everything that individuals and communities do that proclaims and promotes the importance of God, everything that deepens and demonstrates the worth that God has to God's people. This happens in Sunday Schools and small groups. It happens in fellowship dinners and work days at the church. It happens in prayer meetings and hospital visits and funerals and weddings and any time the Body of Christ gathers to be the Body of Christ. One important aspect of worship is mission, which we will explore in more detail below. Here, however, we will confine ourselves to the way a worshipping community creates the context for the entire sanctification of individuals by offering corporate encounters with God through word and deed, proclamation and sacrament.

Word and Worship

There is a truth about human existence that every parent and child knows: we demonstrate how important something is to us by how much attention we give it. Parents want their children to listen to them, and doing so allows the child to demonstrate love and respect. Children want parents to pay attention to them, and doing so allows parents to convey worth and value. Especially in cultures where bright and noisy distractions are always and everywhere available, paying attention to something is a clear demonstration of its importance.

When the church gathers for a service of worship, they gather to pay attention and express that attention in words. First, there are words that the gathered community says and sings to focus its attention on God. These are words that celebrate God's character and majesty, God's acts of deliverance, and the hope that God gives to God's people. In a worship setting, the people speak because God is paying attention, and they respond to that by focusing their own attention through prayers, praise, and proclamation. They also respond by confessing the ways they have failed to pay attention to God, repenting of the gap between who they are and who God has called them to be. As a group of people bring their separate attentions to a single focal point, a community emerges from that collection of individuals. This is true with any focus—a common goal, a common location, or a common history—but in worship the church enacts this unity in a special way. By coming together and using words to celebrate God's worth, they prepare themselves to hear the words that God uses to convey the things God deems worthwhile.

For most Protestant Christians, the proclamation of God's word through Scripture is the focal point of a worship gathering. Off and on throughout the service—often especially near the end—the congregation moves from attentive speaking to attentive listening. They move from articulating their affirmation of God's worth to demonstrating God's worth by placing themselves under the authority of what God wants to say. This is a fundamental expression of what it means for us to consecrate ourselves fully to God and for God to set us apart entirely for God's purposes in the world. One cannot serve purposes that one knows nothing about, and we cannot act as God's agents in the world until God teaches us what that means. We learn that by paying attention. We can and should read the Bible on our own, but it is only in community that those words take on flesh. It is in community that we learn how God wants us to act, learn what God considers to be important, learn what it means to live as Christ lived. This learning is more than information; it is formation. Because it happens in community, it changes who we are, not just what we know. By expressing our worship to God in words and by listening to God's words in worship, we become more and more the people God is calling us to become.

Sacraments as Invitations to Sanctification

For most Catholic Christians, the focus point of worship is the celebration of the sacraments. Many evangelical groups, however, struggle to understand why sacraments are important and what they mean. This struggle often arises from a worry that using physical objects in worship can easily become idolatry, drawing our worship toward things in this world rather than directing it to the God Who Is Beyond. While that is a legitimate concern—idolatry remains a constant temptation for God's people—it must be balanced by the recognition that God created a good world whose very nature was designed to point back toward God. Entire sanctification is about how human lives can be tangible and physical reflections of God's intangible and spiritual nature. That means we should give some attention to the way our sacramental encounters with God foster this work. After all, God offered grace to the world in a tangible way in Jesus, and the church is called upon to continue that offering as the Body of Christ tangibly present in the world (see below).[2] So, it makes sense for the church's own encounters with God to include tangible reminders and representations of grace as well.

As communal and composite creatures, we human beings often symbolize our important relationships in physical ways. Nations create flags to represent their country, and pledging allegiance to those flags displays and reinforces the patriotism of its citizens. Couples exchange rings during a wedding ceremony, embodying their commitments to each other into wearable symbols that become a part of everything they do from then on. These symbols not only help us stay mindful of the fundamental relationships that shape our activity, they actually make those relationships stronger. That same dynamic, then, can be seen in the way sacraments function in the church's worship of God.

First through the waters of baptism and thereafter through the bread and the wine of communion, we express and extend our devotion to God in physical ways. To be entirely devoted to God, we must make God a part of everything that we do. What better way to symbolize that than by eating and drinking the representations (i.e., "presenting to us again") of Christ's broken body and shed blood. Sanctification is about living as a representation of Christ, and we become more mindful that Christ fills us and empowers us spiritually when we celebrate that filling and empowering physically. By recognizing our dependance on God in this way, we demonstrate to ourselves and others how important God is to us; we "worth-ship" God. Because this is an act of "communion," the very same sacrament that celebrates our dependance on Christ also celebrates our interdependence on one another. It is hard to imagine a better

---

2 For more on this idea, see Karl Rahner, *The Church and the Sacraments* (London: Herder and Herder, 1963).

medicine for sin-sick, self-addicted people to take than one that celebrates how much God loves them and calls them to love one another. So, we symbolically consume the body of Christ in church in order to be becoming together the Body of Christ in the world, which leads us to the idea of mission.

Church as Holy, Missional Community

Being entirely set apart for God is not a passive affair. God does not restore God's image in us so that our soul shines nicely on a shelf in heaven. God transforms and sanctifies the followers of Christ so that they become God's active agents in the world that God made and is redeeming. Thus, as a sanctified and sanctifying community, the church is also a holy, missional community. Holiness has always been about displaying God's nature and character to the world. It is about showing everyone else a picture of God that makes them want to be a part of God's new creation project themselves.

In the Old Testament, transformative encounters with the Holy God are always linked to the accomplishment of God's purposes in the world. Moses is given an experience of God's holy presence so that he would be empowered to lead the people of God to the Promised Land (Ex 33-34). Isaiah is given a vision of the Holy God in the temple so that his own sins might be purged and he might volunteer to be an emissary to God's people (Is 6:1-8). Even when God comes to Elijah as a "gentle whisper" that follows the wind and earthquake and fire, the encounter is designed to revive Elijah's flagging spirits so that he could once again resume his role as God's agent in Judah and Israel (1 Kgs 19:11-18). God displays God's nature so that it might transform God's people so that they, too, might display God's nature as they further God's work in the world. This dynamic links holiness, sanctification, and mission in the church as well.

The first time the word "church" appears in the canonical order of the New Testament is on the lips of Jesus. Following up on Peter's confession of him as the Christ in Matthew 16, Jesus says:

> And I tell you that you are Peter, and on this rock I will build
> my church, and the gates of Hades will not overcome it. I will
> give you the keys of the kingdom of heaven; whatever you bind
> on earth will be bound in heaven, and whatever you loose on
> earth will be loosed in heaven. (Mt 16:18-19)

Matthew introduces the idea of the church to his readers by reminding them that the church is an extension of Jesus's own work and ministry. The community that will emerge from the sanctifying fires of Pentecost will be a community that Jesus builds, and it is a community with marching orders. We sometimes read this passage with the idea that the church is a fortress that protects its members from the attack of God's enemies, but the movement implied by the passage is exactly the opposite. Gates do not move, so it is not that the gates of Hades are attacking the church. Instead, the church is seen as the one on the assault, laying siege to the kingdom of death and darkness, whose gates are not strong enough to keep them out. The image of the church Jesus gives here is an active and missional one.

Jesus further reinforces this proactive vision of the church by saying that he will give to Peter a set of keys. These keys are to be used to unite the work of heaven and earth, in line with the way Jesus had taught his disciples to pray in Matthew 6:10. Empowered and commissioned by Jesus, the church's job is to go about unlocking all of the cages that keep God's world from flourishing as it was designed to flourish and locking up anything that stands in the way of that project. This, of course, was the essence of Jesus's own ministry as well.

Paul, too, reflects on the church as a continuation of the Incarnation. He does this by exploring the idea that the church as the "Body of Christ" in Romans 12 and 1 Corinthians 12. Paul uses the image of a body to say several different things about the church, the first being that the church continues the work that God began in Jesus. Bodies are centers of activity, designed to do things. When Paul introduces this idea to the Romans, he follows it with a long list of imperatives, exhorting the Roman church to do the things that God has gifted them to do (Rom 12:6-21). Some of these have to do with the way members of the church serve each other, others with the way the church displays God's values to the world, but all of them require that the church be active. Nowhere does Paul portray the church as if it were a safe place to hide until Jesus returns. As the Body of Christ, the church is God's primary physical agent of salvation and sanctification in the world now as Jesus was during his time on earth. So, as Paul encourages his readers in Galatia, "Let us not become weary in doing good, for at the proper time we will reap a harvest if we do not give up. Therefore, as we have opportunity, let us do good to all people, especially to those who belong to the family of believers" (Gal 6:9-10).

In 1 Corinthians, Paul spends more time exploring this body metaphor for what it says about the way differences in the church work together toward their common mission. Paul says, "Now to each one the manifestation of the Spirit is given for the common good" (1 Cor 12:7). As in Pentecost, the Spirit of God "inspires" the Body of Christ by breathing life into it. That life is expressed in various functions, all of which are designed to work together so that the church reflects the love that is God's central characteristic (1 Cor 13). The body works all together, or it does not work at all. It is in the loving community that arises from the bond of the Spirit that God's nature and character is most fully displayed.

Once again we see that holiness and sanctification are essentially communal realities. This is no surprise since they represent on one level the restoration of the image of God in us that is our communal creaturehood, our reflection of the God who is a Trinitarian community of love. God empowers this work in both communities and individuals through a baptism of the Holy Spirit, and God nurtures it through the community's life of worship and mission. When the church functions as it was intended, it shows the world what God is like and it shapes the world to be more and more like the world God created it to be.

Chapter Nine

The Sanctified Life: Perfecting The Image

We have seen that entire sanctification means giving God our unqualified "yes." Like a commitment to marriage, this "yes" opens up for us a whole new realm of relational possibilities—with God, with other people, and even with the rest of God's creation. Just as a marriage is not a task to be accomplished but a relationship to be nurtured and deepened, so, too, is our committed relationship to God. Those who are entirely about the business of being sanctified find themselves on a journey, an adventure of grace, as God turns that grounding commitment into a life that ever more deeply mirrors God's own life.

This means that the sanctified life must be seen as a dynamic life, a life in which we are always becoming more and more the person God created us to be. While our commitment is anchored in a moment, our perfecting—our maturity—takes time to develop. As we journey with God, God reveals new things to us about how our life can be more "conformed to the image of [God's] Son" (Rom 8:29). This requires us to confess the ways in which we have not yet been perfected and respond in obedience to this new light that we are given. God shows us new opportunities that we can take in order to be more effective agents for God in the world, opportunities we may have missed in the past. So, we ask forgiveness for those missed chances and then proactively pursue the ones God has now put in front of us. Far from being the culmination of our spiritual renewal, entire sanctification is the place where we kick our image-of-God recovery into high gear, the place where our sanctification begins in earnest. When we are entirely about the business of becoming like God, we can celebrate the victories God has empowered even as we yearn for the further work to be done. As Paul confesses to the Philippians:

> Not that I have already obtained all this, or have already arrived at my goal [*i.e., been made perfect*], but I press on to take hold of that for which Christ Jesus took hold of me. Brothers and sisters, I do not consider myself yet to have taken hold of it. But one thing I do: Forgetting what is behind and straining toward what is ahead, I press on toward the goal to win the prize for which God has called me heavenward in Christ Jesus. (Phil 3:12-14)

There is no way that we could lay out all of the implications of this sanctified life, and each of our spiritual journeys is as unique as we are. However, there are some common threads that we can trace that give us a general idea how this perfecting process works. In the last chapter, we considered some of the implications of the sanctified life for recapturing our communal creaturehood in the church. Here we will explore a few other ways in which the life of entire sanctification is a life dedicated to the restoration of God's image in us as composite creatures, laboring stewards, and moral creatures. We will also briefly discuss the difficult question of whether or not our full commitment to God's sanctifying work in our lives can be lost.

Embodied Holiness

God created human beings to be physical representations of God's image and likeness, and entire sanctification is very much a physical reality. Far from being an abstract condition of our immaterial soul, entire sanctification reshapes our material life in every way—so much so that "disembodied" sanctification is no sanctification at all.

To begin with, that addiction to ourselves that we call sin has shaped our brain, its desires, and its responses to the world in radically selfish ways. We want things that satisfy us and make us feel good. We feel anger and fear and shame when the world is threatening us or not going the way that we want it to. Those intuitive biological impulses enslave us, and none of them look much like God. They are a part of us, however, and they remain with us after our conversion and sanctification experiences as constant temptations to turn back to our self-addiction. As we learn to live as reflections of God's loving nature and character, we need to reprogram those reactions and desires so that they are more aligned with God's. God has equipped us with a biology that is as capable of feeling affection as it is of feeling hate, empathy as much as anger, compassion as much as fear. Our biology can be trained to actively want the good of others more than our own good. Entire sanctification involves confessing the places where our self-oriented biology asserts itself and then taking the opportunities God gives us to learn to want what God wants. This usually means acting beyond our emotions until we train them to be more oriented toward God's values.

Sometimes this looks like suppressing our intuitive biological reactions to disappointments and hurts and asking God to teach us how to react lovingly until those loving reactions become a part of who we are. As we refuse to follow through with our selfish emotions, their tempting force in our lives weakens. That leaves room for more holy tempers to arise in their place. Sometimes this looks like treating people in the most wisely loving manner we can think of—even when we don't really like them—until God develops in us a genuine, empowering, felt love for them. Fostering our unselfish emotions— affection, empathy, compassion—often involves putting ourselves in situations where we don't feel anything but still act in love until those feelings arise. Whatever particular form it takes, embodied holiness means practicing being human in the way that God was human in Jesus. By God's grace, that likeness eventually becomes a "natural" part of our identity and we react to the world in godly ways without even thinking about it.

Another part of learning how to reflect God more and more in our physical frame involves taking seriously Paul's admonition to the Corinthians: "Do you not know that your bodies are temples of the Holy Spirit, who is in you, whom you have received from God? You are not your own; you were bought at a price. Therefore honor God with your bodies" (1 Cor 6:19-20). Paul makes that claim while discussing sexual immorality, but the idea that God desires our bodies to be physical locations that invoke the presence of the Holy Spirit has wide implications. We saw in the last chapter how sacraments become physical representations of God's grace. What would happen if we treated our bodies "sacramentally"? What if we lived our physical life as if our flesh was the very thing that God wants to use to become more tangibly present and active in the world? Entire sanctification involves taking seriously the idea that God wants our "dust" to point toward God just as much as our "breath" does.

Sometimes this looks like a basic concern about health and fitness. We will simply be better agents for God in the world, better physical representatives of God's loving character, if our bodies function as efficiently as our circumstances allow. Many of our self-addicted behaviors involve the indulgence of our biological appetites, and this is why the church has always seen gluttony and sloth as among the deadliest of sins. This is also one reason why holy people have largely avoided pleasure-oriented chemicals like recreational drugs or alcohol. Self-oriented behaviors have no place in the sanctified life because there is simply no way to get high or get drunk lovingly. As God sets us more and more apart for God's purposes in the world, we confess our selfish indulgences and learn to be more disciplined with our bodies. That way, we will have more energy to devote to God's Kingdom. If we "are not our own," as Paul reminds us, then our stewardship of God's created order (see below) begins with the part of creation we are most intimately connected with—our bodies.

Sometimes, however, this looks quite different. Sometimes, the entire sanctification of our bodies shows up in how we react when our bodies do not function the way they should. Being creatures of dust, we get hurt and get sick, and eventually our bodies wear out and we die. However, if Jesus is our example of what a human life entirely consecrated to God looks like, then we know God can shine through our lives in even our suffering. In fact, that is often the place where others see God in us most clearly. The pagan centurion near Jesus's cross sees God in the way Jesus met his death (Mk 15:39). Paul notes how God's power in his life is "made perfect in weakness" (2 Cor 12:9), and so he can look forward to even the painful ways in which his physical life points to God. To the Colossians he says, "Now I rejoice in what I am suffering for you, and I fill up in my flesh what is still lacking in regard to Christ's afflictions, for the sake of his body, which is the church" (Col 1:24). The sanctification of our dust often looks like suffering well—suffering redemptively and lovingly—because entire sanctification looks like Jesus.

Finally, God wants God's physical image-bearers to display God's nature and character beyond their individual physicality. We are communal creatures as well as composite ones, and our physical life is a life we live together. Entirely sanctified persons strive to reflect the divine life in the way they participate in all of the tangible realities of human corporate life. The institutions that shape communal life are dust-bound and temporary in the same way that human bodies are. Political and economic institutions rise and fall, but Jesus's followers are still called to engage them in sanctified ways. Corporately, we repent of the ways our communal life inhibits love, and we pursue better ways of living that promote it. The symbols and values of a culture are always given tangible expression in art and music and literature and dance and food and celebrations and the like, and those who have been set apart for God in this world will use those things to display God's image to the world. Entire sanctification involves living for God in a physical world that God created to be good. There is, therefore, no facet of authentic human life that cannot be sanctified and made to serve God's purposes.

Sometimes this looks like a redemptive engagement with the structures and systems of society, getting involved and making the kind of difference that points to God. It could mean voting in loving and informed ways but also treating one's political opponents as God's image-bearers as well. It could mean founding businesses designed to further the good of all and running those businesses in ways that reflect God's priorities rather than selfish ones. It could even mean sculpting an image or shooting a film that raises deep questions about the real meaning of human life.

Sometimes, however, the structures of society are so sinful and self-oriented that they cannot be made to point to God. In this case, sanctification often looks like standing apart from them and pointing out the ways in which they dehumanize people instead of empowering them. In these cases, sanctification often looks like a prophetic disengagement from the world. This is especially true when God is more clearly seen in the difference between how a fallen world works and how God has called humanity to live. That could mean lovingly protesting broken political systems rather than endorsing them. It could also mean staying away from certain businesses or companies because the way they do business hurts people rather than helps them.

Living, then, as entirely sanctified composite creatures means taking our bodies and brains and societies seriously and doing everything we can to ensure that our physical lives point to God. In this way, the image of God in us is restored in deeper ways. Our lives become clearer reflections of the divine life, and we become more effective agents for God in the world.

Sacred Stewardship

Reflecting on the importance of our physicality in entire sanctification naturally leads us to a deeper reflection on our role as stewards of God's physical world. Our self-focus and sin have led us fallen human beings to use the world and the things in it in selfish and consumptive ways. Entire sanctification leads us to repent from such ways and recover the role that God had created humans to play in God's creation: working in the world to make it better and taking care of the creation that God has entrusted to us (Gen 2:15).

Our God is a creative God who is always at work in the world to bring out its good potentials. Those who have entirely devoted themselves to showing the world what God looks like are going to be an eager part of that creative and "new creative" work. They will seek out opportunities to improve the world and the lives of those in it however their circumstances allow. Sanctified individuals live as producers more than as consumers—giving more than they take—because that is the kind of life that reflects God. They live as those concerned more with the betterment of others than themselves, serving them and helping them to flourish even when that involves significant personal sacrifice. In other words, they live in ways that look like the Son of Man, who "did not come to be served, but to serve, and to give his life as a ransom for many" (Mt 20:28).

Lives that add value to the world and to other people vary widely in their shape and form, depending on the gifts and graces God bestows and the callings God gives. There are those who are gifted and called to work in the world of business. They create products and offer services that improve the quality of people's lives, and they empower others to earn a livelihood for themselves and their families. There are those who are gifted and called to work in the fields of science and technology, discovering more and more truth about God's created order. They can then put that truth to work in ways that improve creation, helping it to flourish and helping human beings to flourish within it. There are others who create art that adds to the beauty and meaning of the world and still others who serve and protect their fellow human beings as janitors and waiters, as police officers and firefighters, as teachers and secretaries and clerks and assistants. All work that fosters the good ordering of God's creation is sanctified work because all such work ultimately points back to God.

In talking about "sanctified work," however, we must always remember the Sabbath principle we explored back in chapter two. Our work points back to God best when it is an expression of who we are in God. "Holy doing" comes from "holy being." The work of those who are completely committed to God tends to look less like duty and more like delight, less a matter of "have to" and more a matter of "get to." Because God has freed us up from our addiction to ourselves, we are free to serve others in all that we do. Sanctified work is joyful and cheerful work even when it is difficult and costly because it is the work of those being made ever more perfect in love.

In our day and age, another inescapable implication of entire sanctification is the sacred stewardship of our planet. We who bear the image of God must see our role in the natural world as one of care-taking "dominion" (Gen 1:26, 28 KJV) rather than exploitive "domination." The sacred work to which we have been called is more than a work with other human beings; it is a work with all of God's creation. Issues of the environment and humanity's role in it are often fraught with political overtones, and a group of truly sanctified Christians may well disagree about the best policies to pursue or laws to pass that would foster the best relationship between humans and the rest of creation. However, they would not disagree that this is the goal they should pursue.

No one who is entirely about the business of reflecting God is going to look at the world as a possession to be used and discarded because that is not how God treats it. God cares for the birds and the grass (Mt 6:26-30) and cares about letting even animals rest on the Sabbath (Ex 20:10). God gives fields a break from human farming practices (Ex 23:10-11, Lev 25:4) and mourns the way human sin pollutes the land (Is 24:5, Jer 2:7). God knows that all of creation is suffering because of human sin (Rom 8:19-21), and God's new creation project encompasses everything that God has made—not merely those creatures God created in God's image (Is 65:17-25, Rev 21:1). Those who have been entirely set apart for God ought to be those most sensitive to the ways in which God's creation has been misused, and they will often be the voice of repentance and confession for a human race that so often fails at its creational stewardship.

Once we allow God and God's agenda to completely capture our attention, we can no longer use the world God has created for purely selfish ends. We will still need to eat and clothe ourselves. We have to make shelters to live in and use the resources of the world to promote human life. All of that, however, serves the purpose of our being redemptive agents in God's world, and all that work must be done in a way that honors God and reflects God's nature and character. The way we reflect God by stewarding God's world will vary widely according to our situation, but there is no option for us not to do it. There is no way for us to point effectively toward God with our lives and disregard the goodness that God sees in everything that God made.

Sanctified Morality

God created human beings to be moral creatures. They are oriented toward the good of God's world, and they flourish within the boundaries God established for them. In their self-focus and sin, however, human beings disregard God's laws and boundary lines. So, they fall into shame and cycles of malfunction that they cannot fix themselves. When God restores human beings to fellowship, they begin to live again as God had created them to live, and that changes their attitude toward God's laws. Entire sanctification entails a new appreciation of the wise way in which God maps out the clearest path to our best good. Entirely sanctified people are concerned with more than staying inside the boundary lines and resisting the temptation to sin. They actively seek out the best structures and conditions that help them maximize their relationship to God and their effectiveness as God's agents in the world. To use our marriage analogy again, complete devotion is more than a refusal to date other people once we are married; it is an active seeking of the best way to stay in love with our spouse and fall in love with them over and over again.

One of the besetting sins of holiness traditions is legalism. Legalism is what happens when religious people begin to care more about *where* God draws the boundary lines than *why* God draws them. In other words, legalism focuses more on the negative behaviors that law prevents than on the positive ones that obedience empowers. In such cases, the call to holiness is reduced from a desire to reflect God into the world to a concern about keeping a set of laws, which are then extended and interpreted to cover every dimension of human life. Concerns about human flourishing are buried under the weight of tradition and detail, and laws begin to oppress people rather than liberate them. Such situations do not reflect the God of love, and they are just as likely to work against God's purposes for the world as for them.

Jesus confronts this attitude when he encounters it in his ministry. Some of the Pharisees were more concerned about protecting the Sabbath than about protecting human beings from oppression, which was one reason why God gave the Sabbath in the first place (Mk 2:23-3:6, see Deut 5:12-15). They too often reduced holiness to ritual behavior instead of seeing it as a chance to reflect God (Mk 7:1-20). Jesus corrects their misunderstandings by reminding them that "The Sabbath was made for man, not man for the Sabbath" (Mk 2:27), indicating that human flourishing was more important than human-made boundary lines. He also sums up all the commandments into the idea of loving God and loving one's neighbor (Mk 12:28-31). Furthermore, he emphasizes the true freedom that is found in following God and being a member of God's family: "So if the Son sets you free, you will be free indeed" (Jn 8:36).

The life of a fully devoted Jesus follower, then, is a life of freedom, not bondage. It prioritizes people over boundary lines even while it recognizes that true freedom is only found within the limits that God prescribes. Jesus celebrated the fact that God reveals the contours of a life that reflects God, and most of the Sermon on the Mount is dedicated to showing how God's boundaries lead to human flourishing (Mt 5-7).[1] As a result, sanctified people joyfully accept God's freedom-giving boundary lines because they know them to be reliable guidelines for loving people and for protecting the things that matter to God. At the same time, sanctified people are also very aware of the way in which even accidental and unintentional missteps over those boundary lines can impede love, and they are quick to confess and repent of them.

Paul reflects this sanctified view of law when he calls people to live wholeheartedly toward God's purposes and even go beyond what the law requires them to do. He asks Philemon to free Onesimus, even though Philemon had every right to keep him as a slave (Phm 12-17). He recognizes that there are many things that are permitted but which are not beneficial or constructive (1 Cor 10:23). In fact, Paul tells the Corinthians that "No one should seek their own good, but the good of others" (1 Cor 10:24), and he encourages them to voluntarily accept boundary lines for themselves that promote the good of other people (1 Cor 10:25-33). With the Romans, Paul articulates this same attitude as a concern for those whose faith is weak (Rom 14:1-23). In both cases, Paul exhorts his readers to see their freedom in Christ as an opportunity to love and do good, not something for them to selfishly protect.

A sanctified approach to morality, then, is driven by a concern to maximize the good of others instead of a selfish concern to figure out what one can "get away with." It voluntarily takes on restrictions if those restrictions benefit others, and it lives above the level of the law by turning the other cheek and going the extra mile (Mt 5:39-41). However, because it is driven by love, it also does not force others to obey. Sanctified obedience is offered as a testimony to the trustworthiness of God and an invitation for others to trust God as well. It does not compel because it is not compelled. As a full recovery of our moral creaturehood, entire sanctification combines

---

1 A particularly helpful exploration of the connection between obedient living and human flourishing can be found in Jonathan T. Pennington, *The Sermon on the Mount and Human Flourishing: A Theological Commentary* (Grand Rapids, MI: Baker Academic, 2017).

the freedom found in following Christ with an earnest desire to use that freedom only in ways that mirror God. Christlike freedom—sanctified freedom—is always a freedom to love.

Sanctification Lost?

As we follow the impulses of God's grace to become more and more like God, we fall more and more in love with God, and that love spills out into a love of our neighbor as well. But what happens if we ignore those impulses? On one level, this seems rather unlikely. In completely committing our lives to God we have decided that God is ultimately trustworthy and that we want the life—and only the life—that God has for us. On the other hand, however, it does seem that there are those who once lived fully for God but who have now wandered away and gotten stuck on themselves again. Can the grace or experience or commitment of entire sanctification be lost?

Once again, our marriage analogy helps us here. Marriages are always commitments to permanence, and we understand them as "once and done" realities. However, we also know that many people do not nurture their commitments and end up seeing them falter as one or both parties prioritize their individuality over their relationship. Marriage is not a magic bullet that kills off our selfishness; it merely creates one of the best environments in which one can learn to be more and more loving. So, too, the grace of God that empowers entire sanctification is not a grace that forces us to behave and conform to God's will. As we have seen above, it is a grace that gives us a new kind of freedom, and freedom always comes with the possibility of using it poorly.

If we think about entire sanctification as a state into which we enter and from which we leave, then it becomes very difficult to determine the boundary line that determines when we've left it. However, if we see entire sanctification as a marriage-like relationship with God, then there are clear signs that one's marriage is in trouble and needs attention. Like all relational realities, we know that they are healthy when they are growing and unhealthy when they are fading. God, of course, is always at work to keep the relationship healthy, and God's end of the relationship is always as committed as it can be. It is possible, however, for us to ignore our end and so to suppress or ignore the invitations to grow along the lines we've outlined above. When that happens, we begin to turn away from God and back to ourselves. If we do that enough, then the addictive nature of our self-interest will eventually kick in, and we will fall back into the divided life we once knew—or even try to run away from God altogether.

This is one more reason to emphasize the active and dynamic nature of the sanctified life and to resist the impulse to see it as a finished work. It is also a reason to keep our lingering weaknesses firmly and confessionally in front of us rather than pretend we are stronger than we are. A marriage in which spouses say "I'm sorry" is likely much stronger than one in which those words never occur, and a confessional relationship to God will always be stronger than one in which repentance is ignored or absent. So long as we are focused on our relationship with God, growing with Christ to be more like Christ, we are in no danger of turning away from him. So long as we give our marriage to God the full attention we promised with our entire consecration, we can be assured that God will use that focus to keep us always on track.

Conclusion

Once upon a time, there was a loving and creative God. This God danced a happy dance of love as a Father and a Son and a Life-Giving Breath. In fact, God had so much love that God decided to share it. So, God made a world. The world was very good, and God loved the world very much. God loved the sound of the birds and the flight of the eagles. God loved the tall trees and the deep oceans. God loved watching mother bears hug their cubs and father monkeys play with their babies. But God had a special love for the people God made because God had made them to be like God. That way, they and God could be good friends because they had so much in common. But friends are only friends because they want to be. So, God let these humans decide if they wanted to be God's friend or not.

Sadly, people decided not to love God and be God's friend. They wanted to love themselves instead, and so they ran away from God. But they forgot that God is love. So, when they ran away from God, they ran away from love. They forgot how to love themselves, and they ended up being very mean to one another.

Happily, God still loved them and chased after them. People didn't like being chased, and they hurt God to make God stop chasing them. But God loved them and chased after them anyway. Some of the people decided to stop running and say they were sorry. God forgave them and reminded them that God still loved them. Because they were loved, they let God teach them how to love again. They realized how wonderful learning to love was, and they decided to spend their whole lives loving God and other people. They even helped God chase down other people who were still running away. The more they ran with God, the more their love grew. The more their love grew, the more people could see it. The more they saw it, the more they wanted to stop running, too. More people said they were sorry, and more people learned how to love and join the chase. Eventually the chase reached everyone it could reach, and everything was filled with love. God and God's people were together again, and they all lived lovingly ever after.

The story of the gospel is, in many ways, quite simple to understand—so simple that we can capture its central dynamic in a children's story. Simple to understand, however, does not mean simple to live out. Living out the gospel takes all that we have, and even that never feels like enough. Fortunately, the gospel also tells us that all of our work is really God's work in and through us, and God is always able to accomplish what needs to be done. Sometimes God works in the world to promote God's Kingdom and the space of God's salvation in ways we humans never could. Sometimes, however, God works through those who follow Jesus to empower them to do things they could never do on their own. Following God-in-Christ, then, involves living in the tension between Jesus's words to his disciples, "Apart from me, you can do nothing" (John 15:5), and Paul's confession to the Philippians: "I can do all this through him who gives me strength" (Phil 4:13). Entire sanctification is one way of labeling a life in which our full surrender to God is joined with God's full empowerment.

In these pages, we have explored a particular way of understanding entire sanctification that resonates with the testimony of Scripture and allows us to see how the pieces of God's nature, human nature, sin, salvation and sanctification all fit together. However, as we noted in the Introduction, this work is only intended to help start discussions about sanctification—not finish them. Attentive readers will likely still have a lot of questions left in their minds, and that is a good thing. God is so much bigger than we humans can understand, and God's work is deeper that we humans can ever know. So, our questions become opportunities for us to keep moving forward, to keep digging deeper and reaching higher. Entire sanctification is more like a new beginning of the Christian journey than the end of it, and our understanding of entire sanctification works the same way. What we know should lead us to seek out what we do not yet know.

In this way, our quest to understand God's work in our lives becomes a part of that very work. The more we know, the more we are empowered to live out what we know. However, it is also true that the more we know, the more we realize how little we understand. There is a mystery to God's work, and that serves to always keep us humble about our knowledge of it. If this book has brought its readers a little closer to that mystery, it has served its purpose. If it invites readers to further explore—and even plunge deeper into—that mystery, then it will have succeeded beyond its author's fondest hope.

"[Now] May God himself, the God of peace, sanctify you through and through. May your whole spirit, soul and body be kept blameless at the coming of our Lord Jesus Christ"
(1 Thes 5:23).

Timothy Crutcher

Timothy Crutcher is the pastor of the Florida Keys Church of the Nazarene. He spent nearly twenty years as a college professor and also served as a missionary in Belgium and Kenya. He has degrees from Southern Nazarene University, Nazarene Theological Seminary, and the Catholic University of Louvain, and he is the author of *John Wesley: His Life and Thought* and *The Crucible of Life: The Role of Experience in John Wesley's Theological Method*. He lives with his family in Key Largo, Florida.